A

AN ISLAND
CALLED SMITH

JON GOWER

First Impression—2001

ISBN 1 85902 983 3

This book is published with the support of the
Arts Council of Wales.

Front and back cover illustrations:
John Hurt Whitehead III

Printed in Wales at
Gomer Press, Llandysul, Ceredigion

I mam
ac i'm nai Ross Dewi Gower –
pegynau pwysig fy mywyd

ACKNOWLEDGEMENTS

This book would be empty were it not for the generosity of the people of Smith Island, who shared their time and their stories with me. I wouldn't have got there were it not for the John Morgan award, and I am hugely grateful to the trustees for allowing me to cross the Atlantic in order to flesh out an interest kindled by a single newspaper article. Thanks too to Sir Jeremy Isaacs for writing the foreword. They say ask a busy man . . .

As I am the last recipient of such an award, I should like to thank those friends of the great Welsh journalist who established the award in his memory and enabled books by the likes of Lewis Davies, Robert Minhinnick, Nigel Jenkins and Patrick Dobbs to be written.

Francesca Rhydderch, my editor at Gomer, weeded out clumsy phrasing and added punctuation, and did so with good humour and keen-eyed diligence. Diolch o galon iti.

The Arts Council of Wales kindly chipped in, so thanks for their financial support.

I'm also indebted to Julie Barton of BBC Radio Wales for commissioning a radio series to complement this present volume, to Jim Hawes, to Chapter Arts Centre for its support – and for running the best bar in the known universe – and to impresario and enthusiast Peter Florence at the Hay Literary Festival for organising the launch of the book, in the year he added Bill Clinton to the list of Hay luminaries. My excellent friend Emyr Jenkins hosted late night sessions in his kitchen in Rhiwbina and listened to me drone on about an island in America, providing the usual sterling support and interest.

As you will see from the bibliography, my Chesapeake bookshelf groans like the hull of an old skiff under the weight of the many books that have supplied me with information and inspiration: thanks to those authors who have underlined how rich a text is the Chesapeake itself. Invidious as it is to single out one name, it has to be Tom Horton, whose *Island Out of Time* should be read by anyone who enjoyed this volume. They will then meet other islanders and see the place in other seasons.

Jon Gower, Caerdydd, 2001

FOREWORD

'Ask the fellows who cut the hay.'

Ronald Blythe got it right: the best way to take a community's pulse, and record memories of a living past, is to talk to people about their work.

Smith Island, in Chesapeake Bay between Maryland and Virginia, is a far cry from East Anglia, or from Wales for that matter – but the dictum holds. Jon Gower, last in a fruitful line of beneficiaries of the John Morgan Writing Award, had the good idea of staying on Smith and, before it is too late, getting to know its inhabitants—very many of them Welsh in origin—declining in number as the sea encroaches and the coastline behind grows nearer and noisier. The result is a sharp, vivid portrait of a salty place, and the men and women who, like their fathers and mothers and grandparents before them, earn their living there.

What they know about on Smith is crabs. They catch them for a living. Jon Gower has a keen eye for landscape, and a sympathetic ear for speech. He is a good listener, and can tell us, in authentic speech, much we never knew of crabs, male and female, young and old, hard- and soft-shelled. (Did you know—I never did—that a soft-shelled crab was in fact a hard-shelled crab that has just shed its skin?) At any rate, the islanders, men and women – potting, landing, picking, shucking, packing and despatching – live by them.

On the gravestones of west Wales, in Cardigan say, or Aberystwyth, I was always struck by the simple statement at the headstone's top of what Evans or Jones or Llewellyn did for a living; mason, butcher, carpenter, wheelwright, master mariner. On Smith Island, the Evanses call themselves 'watermen'. Wind-beaten, brine-encrusted, they went out, they go out still, in every weather, to supply the restaurant tables of cities near and far. For generations they have been born on Smith, schooled on Smith, have married on Smith, worshipped on Smith, died here and been buried here. They ply a good trade, and live a good life.

Will that way of life survive? Yes, for a while at least. In this admirable book though, against the day of change that may be coming, Jon Gower has captured a sense of community, and shows it to us living in these pages.

Smith Island is its own place, but the men and women who live and work there have lessons for us all.

Jeremy Isaacs
April, 2001

Chapter 1

THE ALLURE OF ISLANDS

Land lies in water; it is shadowed green.
Shadows, or are they shallows, at its edges
showing the line of long sea-weeded ledges
where weeds hang to the simple blue from green.

Elizabeth Bishop

Islands are peppered on the map of the human imagination, just as they are on the map of the world – from the sunken islands of the Atlantic to the beatific isle of Avalon. Viewed from space, the great continents look like an archipelago of islands. They symbolise isolation, separateness and solitude. As Rachel Carson put it: 'Islands have always fascinated the human mind. Perhaps it is the instinctive response of man, the land animal, welcoming a brief intrusion of earth in the vast, overwhelming expanse of sea.'

It was the distinctiveness of the Galapagos which sowed the seeds of Charles Darwin's notion of evolution. Others have become renowned sites of incarceration – Alcatraz, Devil's Island, Sing-Sing. Some islands represent those 'floating signifiers' of which Claude Lévi-Strauss wrote when he argued that, in culture, there is always a need for certain concepts and expressions which soak up any excess of existence which has not yet been turned into words.

Possessed by a *horror vacui*, old mapmakers filled the vast spaces of the oceans with their make-believe, as with the dozens of islands such as Mayda which appeared on the map of the North Atlantic but were, in truth, as fantastical as the Phoenix. Other seas also have their imaginary islands. People long believed in Dougherty Island, which lay to the south of

Australia, and sailors sometimes even 'found' it at its given coordinates. One Captain White, following a delusional course, actually sailed round the nonexistent rock. A sighting of the long reported Podesta Island, way off the Chilean coast, came from a man whose name seems strangely apposite in the circumstances – Captain Pinocchio.

In 1932 a clutch of American astronomers decided that Sarah Ann Island, then part of the Gilbert Island group, would be the perfect site to observe a total eclipse of the sun. But an even longer shadow was cast over their plan when they failed to find the island itself. Two other places that exist only on the boundless map of the imagination are Macy's Island and Swain's Island, set in the sea southwest of Tierra del Fuego. A persistent belief in their existence means that they still appear in the Soviet Atlas of the Pacific Ocean.

As a child who enjoyed nothing better than extravagant adventures in the local library, I visited *Treasure Island*, moved on to Ballantyne's *Coral Island* and marooned myself with Alexander Selkirk, a.k.a. Robinson Crusoe. I also observed the challenges to civilisation addressed in William Golding's *Lord of the Flies* – a novel of the marooned which predates that more recent bestseller, Alex Garland's *The Beach*, by almost half a century, and owes much itself to *Coral Island*.

Fired up by my early literary enthusiasms, I found an opportunity at the ripe old age of thirteen to live for a brief while on an island – a terrific opening as a 'shearwater slave', capturing shearwaters for scientific study – banding and the like. Half the world's population of these extraordinary birds – so very much like little albatrosses and able to fly through the tunnel made when a big wave folds over on itself – live on the red sandstone island of Skokholm off the southwestern tip of Wales. Nocturnal birds, they scythed and swooped through the night air, their cries among the ghastliest sounds of nature, described by that fine naturalist R.M. Lockley as being 'like the crow of a throaty rooster whose head is chopped off before the last long note has fairly begun'.

2

That was where my fascination with birds began. Events have subsequently taken me to the holy island of Bardsey, where 20,000 saints are reputedly buried – and then to Aegean islands full of cyclamens in autumn and the perfect whistling notes of golden orioles in spring, and to track down Caribbean birds on islands such as Antigua. And then there was Smith, an island in the U.S.A.'s Chesapeake Bay that, by current estimates, has only twenty years left before being claimed by the sea, an island, therefore, that will disappear in my own lifetime . . .

A traveller in a different place altogether had this to say about the islands he visited: 'Each island is a distinct and idiosyncratic entity, a civilisation, or the reverse, fortuitous in its origins and empirical in its development. There is no rule that holds good beyond the shores of each one unless the prevalence of oddity, the unvarying need to make exceptions to any known rule, can be considered a unifying principle.' One quality of islands is that their very separateness can keep change at bay. As John of Gaunt says of Britain in *Richard II*, – 'This fortress built by Nature for herself/Against infection and the hand of war.'

Smith Island has kept change at bay and is a sort of fortress, a floating marshland, set at several removes from the madhouse which is the twentieth century, so much so that it offers a lifeline, a glimpse of how things might have been, had the great god Capital not held sway, and if noise and pace and rabid consumerism hadn't won the day on the mainland.

Chapter 2

AN ISLAND CALLED SMITH

... a faire Bay compassed but at the mouth with fruitful and delightsome land. Within is a country that may have the prerogative over the most pleasant places of Europe, Asia, Africa or America, for large and pleasant navigable rivers. Heaven and earth never agreed better to frame a place for man's habitation.

Captain John Smith, *Description of Virginia*

The lady taxi driver taking me to catch the ferry to Smith Island – the last inhabited island in Maryland – had this to say as we neared the port of Crisfield: 'You must like water. There's a whole lot of water out there.' She pointed with her cigarette.

There *is* a whole lot of water in the Chesapeake, an estimated eighteen trillion gallons of the stuff. All varieties of water, from turgid muddy water too murky for a terrapin to navigate, to water the colour of champagne, running crystal clear from distant mountainsides. If you managed to drain the entire tidal system – much as Saddam Hussein drained the marshlands of Southern Iraq or Stalin left the entire Aral Sea dry – *and* you managed the considerable civil engineering feat of stoppering the twelve-mile wide ocean mouth, it would take more than a year before all the rivers, streams and annual storm run-off could fill the huge basin. Here, there is water in great measure.

As the taxi left behind the billboards and motel strip of Salisbury, the land appeared to be flattened by a weight of grey sky and trees gave way to marsh grasses which stretched away, waving like corn. I was reminded of Willa Cather's description of the Nebraska plains in her novel *My Antonia* – 'As I looked about me I felt that the grass was the country, as the water is the sea. The red of the grass made all the great prairie the colour of wine stains, or of certain seaweeds when they are first washed up. And there was so much motion in it; the whole country seemed, somehow, to be running.' Just as the Nebraskans harvest wheat, so too did the early settlers of the Chesapeake reap the seven-foot high marsh vegetation, using Spartina grass to feed their livestock and thatch their roofs.

We were crossing the Delmarva peninsula (a place-name that conflates Delaware, Maryland and Virginia) and water lay everywhere. It snaked and rolled so that wide creeks looked from a distance like silver threads woven into the pattern of the flat landscape. The warning colours of rising willets – a striking black, grey and white – accompanied by the descanting cries of the birds – 'kay-ee', which is one of the early warning systems of the marshes – startled the swamplands. This was a horizontal landscape, subject to that optical illusion that suggests that the sea is somehow higher than the land.

Here, fingers of land and sea became interlocked. As that elegant evoker of the Smith, Tom Horton, put it: 'it is hard to imagine a place where the water twines more intimately with the land, with dozens of rivers and thousand of creeks; where the depths are as moderate, the tides as minimal, the sea heights as kindly . . .'

The Chesapeake is the biggest bay in the USA, covering a gargantuan 2,500 square miles. It has more miles of shoreline than the entire West Coast – its crenellated, crimped and corrugated edges extending for a total of 9,000 miles – edges of soft coast, hard coast, indentation, protuberance, neck, beach, cliff and channel. Its edges are gouged and promontoried, with mud banks gleaming like slices of cut liver. There are rocky exposures which force the wind to lift and veer, carrying bald eagles over isolated headlands, and guarding the mouths of inlets which offer safe harbour.

There are twenty-three rivers which empty their waters into the Chesapeake, including from the west the James,

5

Rappahanock, Potomac and Patuxent, and from the east the Wicomico, Nanticoke, Choptank and Chester, while the Bay's watershed covers 64,000 miles, embracing Cooperstown, New York, the Blue Ridge mountains and the Shenandoahs, and even as far as the rim of North Carolina. Between three and twenty-five miles wide, the Chesapeake Bay is also a fabulously shallow estuary. Equipping boats with fathom counters is an ironic act hereabouts as most watermen can gauge the depth by the colour of the water. It is no surprise that local boatbuilders favour a flat-bottomed structure.

The native tribes, and the languages they spoke, persist in the names the English found, still used today for the Bay and its rivers – Chesapeake, Potomac, Patuxent, Patapsco, Susquehanna, Choptank, Nanticoke, Wicomico, Pocomoke, Manokin and Chincoteague. The varied topography is also there in the names – Point Lookout, Piney Point, Cedar Point, Cove Point, Herring Bay, Highland Beach, Sandy Point, Elk River, Turkey Point, Still Pond, Swan Point, Poplar Island, Bar Neck, Rugged Point, Barren Island, South Marsh Island and Terrapin Sound Point.

In her essay 'Nature as Symbol', Mary K. Blair has suggested that, 'in the public mind the Bay is often negative space, geographically fuzzy, lacking the visual unity to become symbolically powerful.' That 'fuzziness' comes with the blurring of edges – water and land, solidity and impermanence, ebb and flow. Yet the Bay remains a powerful symbol, a fecund area of crosscurrents, miraculous migration and evidence of Nature's great restorative powers. Its power and natural forces can be perceived even in a piece of tarmac, in which rivulets of rain gouge the tiniest of channels, moss finds purchase in minute crevices; nature can dismantle even tough man-made materials. Time's attrition can splinter the surface and in those fissures a tiny seed can find sustenance. So too does a study of the Bay show that it has an ability to recover from both disaster and daily poisoning. Just. The Bay might not always be able to heal itself.

The Bay is a continuum of habitats, a gargantuan larder of seafood, or as the writer H.L. Mencken put it, 'a giant protein factory', and the people of Smith Island have learned how to work in this open-air factory by harvesting the grassy acres of widgeongrass which grow in the surrounding waters.

The bounty of the Bay is legendary, and though current harvests have dipped, there has usually been enough food to go around, for osprey, beaver, bass and man. This is the famed Chesepiooc, the 'great shellfish bay' of the Algonquin Indians, As Captain John Smith wrote in his *Description of Virginia*: 'The country is not mountainous nor yet low but such pleasant hills and fertile valleys . . . rivers and brooks, all running most pleasantly into a fair Bay. Of fish we were best acquainted with herrings, rockfish, shad, crabs, oysters . . . and mussels. In summer no place affordeth more plenty of sturgeon, nor in winter more abundance of fowl.'

Yet while crabs are still caught in great numbers, the days when winter waterfowl blotted out the sun and sturgeon streamed through the shallow waters are long gone. To give an idea of the scale of the sturgeon fishery, a report in 1880 estimated that some 320,000 fish were caught on just three rivers – the James, the Potomac and the Rappahannock. The native Americans would capture these enormous fish by lassoing their tails or simply wrestling with them until the fish gave up the ghost. But there are plenty of species taking full advantage of the productivity of an estuary where salt marshes produce nearly ten tons of organic matter per acre per year. Peruse a natural history handbook and look, there is a found poem, a song of abundance!

Whip mud worm and swamp tupelo, umbrella sedge and silky dogwood. Oldsquaw, halberd-leaved tear-thumb, lookdown, windowpane, summer flounder and winter flounder. Florida pompano, northern dwarf tellin, coolie hat snail, alewife, eastern mudminnow and mummichog . . . Whole galaxies of species are revealed: lunar dove shells and moon jellyfish, sun sponge and fossil moon snail, the star coral and the milky ribbon worm, burrowing brittle star, a sunfish called pumpkinseed, a golden star tunicate and the northern stargazer.

There are also macabre hints of death on the mud – the

skeleton shrimps, bloodworms, dead men's fingers, the coffin box bryozoan, a ghost crab and even the requiem shark.

The list goes on and on: the elongated bamboo worm, the eelgrass pill bug, the soft snail fur, the parchment worm crab, the barrel bubble snail, the northern puffer, the lined seahorse, the feather blenny, and what blessed taxonomist named the ponderous ark or the brief squid?

The island passenger boat, the *Jason II* – which began its twice-daily ferry service in 1977 – churned water, the voices of the islanders on board returning home with their mainland shopping going up a register, excitedly. You cross Tangier Sound – named after a nearby island rather than the city in Morocco – to get to Smith. The posts which marked our progress along the main channel – or Big Thoro'fare – guided the eye, registering how the thin charcoal line of the horizon fattened slightly, then became a graph as the marshlands and sporadic trees of Smith Island hove into view. The graph wasn't that agitated, the island has few peaks – made up of clumps of loblolly pines. The loblollies have been described as the palms of the Eastern shore, with their straight scaly trunks rising as much as fifty feet before branching. Other components of the island's arboretum include cedars and bayberries, marking what were once habitations.

An elegant legend has it that the bayberry – which grows in more northerly locales – saved the lives of a great many New England fishermen who would have starved had they not eaten candles made from bayberries which grew wild along the beaches. A thoughtful and philanthropic sea captain, who plied his boat as far as Maryland, paid his thanks for each life saved by planting bayberries along the coast, in the hope that its presence would save lives as it had done before. There was a time when the island was sufficently well wooded for the islanders to name it Woodlands, but by the end of the colonial period the hard woods had been turned into boats and houses. High ground on Smith is only a few feet above sea level. This is a marsh island, a 'spongy archipelago' which has been changing, protozoan-like for years.

8

The ferryboat, the Jason II, plies daily from the small port of Crisfield, which was once the oyster capital of the world. The place has indubitably gone to seed now. In its heyday there were seventy-five oyster-shucking houses, fifty crab-packing plants, four theatres, three bowling alleys, four dance halls and no fewer than twenty-five barber's shops. In those days the resident population of five thousand would triple to fifteen thousand when the oyster-shuckers came to town. If one stands on the barrel pier now, it is difficult to imagine its former busyness, when there were gambling boats and a clutch of speakeasies or 'raw bars' such as the 'Teapot Dome', 'The Sailor's Horn', and the charming 'Bucket of Blood' – a sanguine name if ever there was one.

Though oysters have declined, crabs have remained relatively abundant, clawed creatures which sustain the Smith Island way of life, which can be challenging beyond measure. As one waterman put it, 'The Bay is our provider and protector, our tormentor and sometimes our gaoler when the storms come . . . We follow the water, taking whatever the Bay sends us . . . we never plant anything but we always go and harvest.' The farming comparison is often made about watermen. And they *are* very grateful. Gratitude is often expressed, nowhere more so than at one of Smith's three churches, it being a Methodist island and a place as yet unsullied – well pretty much – by the twentieth century. The Age of Extremes, as the historian Eric Hobsbawn christened it, seems to lour as a cloud over the mainland, with its acres of advertising hoardings, speed cops, and Disneyfication. Smith Island has no bar, no supermarket, or cinema. On the mainland the crab is a buy-a-bucket, make-a-barbeque commodity. On Smith it is a benefaction, a source of income, a way of life. Much as the life of the hunter is so often the very wellspring of culture, so here, the crab is a grail, a sign of God's benificence to him who will venture onto the watery acres of the Bay.

There are many techniques for partaking of its plenty. The list of techniques for getting at its watery treasures make for an extensive catalogue, with all manner of nets being employed – seine, pound and stake gill nets. Then there's eel fishing with pots, gigs and bobs; dredging, patent-tonging and hand-tonging for oysters – catching snapping turtles with hook and line – man's inventiveness as a hunter is everywhere apparent.

*   *   *

As the boat navigated through banks of marsh grass, I noted colour-coded crab floats sprinkled all over the water, marking the position of the pot. Without the crabs there would be no living for the people of Smith, and a visitor would find deserted houses, like those skeletal homesteads that litter the landscape of eastern Montana. Not that every house on Smith is inhabited. Creeping depopulation has been taking its toll, quietly and steadily. Smith, too, has its clapperboard testaments to change – to people moving on, or rather off the island. But there is still a living to be made, and there are crabs to be caught – by the million, in fact, and the Chesapeake Blue Crab has a reputation the world over, and an incredible taste, the mere recollection of which can set off a Pavlovian reaction in anyone who has tried one.

The *Jason* scythed on through waves the colour of old copper. Strange how the colours which best describe the sea are essentially metallic. The sea might be described as pewter, silver, mercury, or lead. That day, close inshore, it was a placid, quicksilver pool. Further out, where a squall licked the water into cat's-paws, the water was like ruckled tin or beaten pewter, an amalgam of crumpled metals. The water, ruffled and disturbed, licked the air with tiny tongues of foam.

As it was May, almost every platform on the navigation pillars was occupied by nesting birds. Ospreys, commonly known as fish hawks, or fishing hawks, are an elegant chocolate brown and cream in colour. They are seemingly omnipresent around the Bay. They fixed us with gimlet eyes as we passed – eyes that can spot a rockfish through refracted water – the x-ray

10

vision of the deadly bird of prey. The marker posts which line the channels on the island approaches make ideal nesting sites, their twiggy edifices holding safe the occasional curious chick which peered over the nest lip. One adult bird flapped slowly away, unperturbed by the boat's engine.

The Chesapeake supports the largest breeding osprey population in the USA with 1500 breeding pairs, which is about twenty per cent of the USA total. The birds return on St. Patrick's Day – or so the watermen say. Ornithologists confirm that the birds do indeed arrive on or near St. Patrick's Day and leave in October. A harbinger of spring, some of the birds will have flown a long way to get here from their winter quarters in Brazil, Colombia and Venezuela. Some even travel as far south as Argentina, and this prodigious feat is summed up in the story, told by banding recovery, of the bird which was ringed as a nestling at Turkey Point, Cecil County in early July, and had reached Brazil by late September. All without a map or compass.

Of all the natural miracles, migration is one of the most inspiring. Young birds, with no map other than genetic blueprint, can find their way across great continents. And find their way back again.

The sight of an osprey hunting is a delight in itself, but to see it catch a fish is to behold a supreme hunter at work. Its eyes spot its prey in the water and adjust to allow for refraction. Then it swoops – the short, sharp spines which cover the base of the foot pad and toes giving it purchase on the wet, wriggling and slippery fish. The talons snap shut in two hundredths of a second; no time for escape.

We passed a disused fishing lodge now commandeered by platoons of double-crested cormorants – which used to be eaten hereabouts – drying out their wings, reptilian in appearance. They looked like those first ever birds, the Archaeopteryx, trying out feathers for the first time in dinosaur skies. There were pelicans too, looking satiated, plump-bellied. It is good fishing round here. Laughing gulls confirmed this, shrieking maniacally. They know.

11

A small flock of dunlin – diminutive waders resplendent in their summer plumage, chestnut-coloured backs and telephone-black bellies, wheeled away in tight formation. These are fly-by-night visitors, birds passing through on their way to nesting grounds on the northern rim of the world. A northern harrier quartered the marshes, floating lazily over the acres of cordgrass. These elegant birds of prey scout around for unsuspecting birds or mammals, then plunge into the reeds, talons agape.

Birdlife is plentiful on and around the Chesapeake. Wildlife likes the borderlands, where two habitats meet and mingle, and in the Bay land meets water, sand meets mud, swamp meets wetter swamp, with all manner of new relationships and connections coming into being as a result. If there is one family of birds that typifies the scene, it is the herons and egrets.

They stood sentinel everywhere. There were great white egrets with long pipe-cleaner necks and the great blue heron, flapping laboriously, its undercarriage seemingly too heavy for it, croaking like a chain smoker. I flipped through the pages of my field guide. This was going to be a testing time for my bird-spotting skills. Pretty much everything I'd ever learned about birds back home, on the other side of The Pond, was redundant here. The names in my Peterson Field Guide seemed merely to underline Bernard Shaw's dictum that the Americans and the British are 'two nations divided by a common language'.

Some of the species we enjoy seeing on both sides of the Atlantic go by different names over here. The great northern diver becomes a common loon, a guillemot is a murre, the brent goose switches a vowel and becomes the brant goose, our widgeon back in Europe is here called the Eurasian widgeon because America has its own widgeon, a common scoter is a black scoter, our goosander is their common merganser, a moorhen is a gallinule, whilst skuas are jaegers. Confused? I was.

We chugged through the last few feet of the main channel or Big Thoro'fare, and the boat tied up at a wooden jetty, at the 'capital' of Smith, the town of Ewell.

There are three towns on Smith – Ewell, Tylerton and Rhodes Point, which used to be called Rogues' Point. Ewell is a place of white houses – which almost automatically evoke comparison with Martha's Vineyard or Nantucket – and has manicured lawns that look as if they've been tended with scissors. The town also has a tall flashing radio mast, taller than anything else on the island by what might as well be a hundred feet. It flicks a pulse of red light at regular intervals.

Ewell comes in two parts – Over the Hill, the part of town which stands above the church, and Down the Field. It is made up of clapperboard houses, mainly arranged in orderly ranks. A torpor hung over the place because of the heat of the day.

The bare bones of the island are as follows: it covers an acreage of 8000 acres but only some 900 are habitable. The island measures eight miles by four miles and is situated roughly ninety-five miles south of Baltimore and twelve miles west of Crisfield.

Water is the principal transport carrier, but that doesn't mean that automobiles are a rare species herabouts. There is, however, only one stretch of paved road, which runs from Ewell to Rhodes Point. There are some who are imaginative enough to describe it as a two-lane road but one thing is certain – it is the shortest state road in Maryland. Certainly the low quality tarmac can be problematic. One summer's day it softened so much that a frail island woman was trapped in it and had to be rescued by two passers-by.

On the island there are three churches, two post offices, one school, three stores, three restaurants – all unlicensed – and 310 boats, which far outnumber automobiles, there being ninety-five cars and trucks, and five school buses. In the absence of police, island cars aren't licensed. Anonymous and rusty wrecks abound, driven until they just fall apart, at which point they are casually abandoned. At one stage, so many of these unsightly old cars littered the island that the inhabitants had to petition the state to dig a trench to bury them. Fifty cars went into the marsh at a cost of 163,000 dollars to the state's taxpayers. Other vital statistics include 180 bicycles,

300 cats (although everyone agrees that this is a very conservative estimate given the fecundity of felines around the place), three fire engines and thirteen golf carts, but no golf course.

I came to Smith because of a newspaper article I once read in the *Times*. In its American news section the paper carried the following headline: *Environmental tide turns against island's heritage: Off the coast of Maryland, a crab fishing community that has its roots in Wales and Cornwall and has endured since 1607 is fighting for survival.*

I have always loved islands and estuaries, so an island set in an estuary with some connections with Wales sounded more than promising. Being what you might call a professional Welshman – delighted by all things connected with this country, which is small enough to hold out the promise of being understood whilst still being big enough to have surprises tucked away around every corner – my appetite was further whetted by reading dusty tomes about America, a country which could never be as neatly summed up as Wales. As I thumbed through books about the history of Maryland, the Welsh connections proliferated, from the names of Maryland rivers such as the Severn and Wye – although these could just as equally have been shipped over from the west of England, as the rivers flow through both Wales and England – to places such as Plimhimmon, a corruption of the Welsh mountain Pumlumon which means 'the five beacons'. Coincidentally, both the Welsh rivers Severn and the Wye have their sources in Pumlumon in mid Wales.

The early Welsh settlers were followed by more recent waves of emigrants, including the miners and their families shipped over to work in the coal mines of Allegany county, in the northwestern corner of the state. The Smith settlers go much further back. One of the Welsh families on Smith, the Evanses, has been living there continuously, since the seventeenth century.

In Maryland, links with Wales appeared in sometimes unexpected places. Take the case of early house chimneys.

14

Early and affluent settlers would erect brick chimneys, but in the absence of enough cash to choose brick they would erect timber or 'Welsh' chimneys. Even these did not come cheap, and, since they were made of wood – four corner posts set into the ground as a framework for shorter timbers set between and all daubed with mud – they were considered a trifle dangerous. Light is shed on the matter in a Somerset county court case, reviewed in 1676, which notes the cost of a Welsh chimney. It was valued at 200 pounds of tobacco, at a time when the assembly of a thirty-foot dwelling cost 1,400, while six days of planing plank was compensated with 240 pounds of tobacco.

Historically, there were sufficient numbers of Welsh people in Tidewater Maryland for St. David's Day, celebrated in just the same way that the Irish marked out St. Patrick's Day and, to a lesser extent, the English St. George's. The Irish and the Welsh made up a greater part of the colonists than is usually recognised: roughly a quarter of the immigrants who left Liverpool for the Chesapeake from 1697 to 1707 were Welsh, and the embarkation port of Bristol drew on the population of nearby south Wales in addition to the West of England.

One colonial celebration was peculiar to the region, namely St. Tamina's Day, usually celebrated on May Day, or the first of May. On St. Tamina's Day the natives wear a piece of buck's tail in their hats, or in some conspicuous position. 'During the course of the evening, and generally in the midst of a dance, the company are interrupted by a sudden intrusion of a number of persons habited like Indians, who rush violently into the room, singing the war song, giving the whoop, and dancing in the style of those people; after which ceremony a collection is made, and they retire well satisfied with the reception and the entertainment'.

I stayed at a small bed and breakfast, the Ewell Tide Inn, where they didn't bother to give me a front door key. They simply don't lock doors hereabouts. Though only a few hours' drive from the cities of the North-East, the crack cocaine of Washington's housing projects, the Beltway and the sprawling creep of cities, the island is many years away, a custodian of old values, its community still rooted in tradition.

Before turning in – the night velvety with squadrons of ghost moths beating themselves senseless against my bedroom window – I read a few pages of John Barth's novel, *Once Upon a Time* which, like so many of his works, takes the Chesapeake as its canvas. 'Neither dry land nor sea, as the Chesapeake is neither salt nor fresh; emblematic equally of stagnation and regeneration, of death and new life ... inbetween lands' which are 'the imagination's mise-en-scène.' I drifted through the inbetweenland separating wakefulness from sleep to the throbbing of boat engines as the watermen prepared for another day on the Bay. It was four o'clock in the morning.

Chapter 3

THE HISTORYMAN

*The poetry of history lies in the quasi-miraculous fact
that once, on this earth, on this familiar spot of ground
walked other men and women as actual as we are
today, thinking their own thoughts, swayed by their
own passions but now all gone . . . gone as utterly as we
ourselves shall be gone like ghosts at cockcrow.*

G.M. Trevelyan

Jennings Evans, the island's remembrancer, has a laugh like
exploding fruit and eyes the colour of clear blue skies. They may
be a little flecked with red now – showing thin veins of life's
sunset – but there is a vitality there that matches his
enthusiasm for his native island. As watermen go, Jennings is
pretty much archetypal. His skin has traces of mahogany,
coloured by whipping wind and searing sun. One imagines his
veins running not with salt water but with brackish Chesapeake
brine. This is not as romantic or far-fetched as it might at first
sound. After all, just as our skeletons are a carry-over from the
calcium-rich oceans of the Cambrian era, so is the *aqua vitae*
which courses through our veins. Our lifeblood is a salty stream
in which sodium, potassium and calcium are present in pretty
much the same cocktail quantities as sea water. This is an
evolutionary carry-over from the days, many aeons ago, when
multi-celled animals developed a circulatory system. Their body
fluid was quite simply the water of the sea. And just to mix
poetry with science, the salinity of the Chesapeake is exactly
that of human tears.

Back in 1872 the Reverend James A. Massey described
Smith islanders as 'almost an amphibious race, for nearly all

the men and boys spend fully half their time on the water.'
Jennings Evans is just such an amphibious creature – a
waterman of long standing. It is a source of great regret to him
that he has had to give up crabbing after many years due to the
ill health.

He is also the island's unoffical historian. Indeed, Smith
seems to be a one-of-everything sort of place: one garbage man,
one telephone lady. So there is one historian, one man who
garners the memories and marshals the tales and Jennings is
he. And as that eminent philosopher of science Karl Popper
once said: 'There is no history, only histories.' So Jennings is
the keeper of the stories. Self-deprecatingly, he describes
himself as 'a museum piece. I used to be a crabber – now they
dust me off to talk to people.'

Jennings sat me down on the porch of the Smith Island
Cultural centre, an institution he was pivotal in creating – a
celebration and consideration of the island's way of life and
history. But as he himself pointed out in a newspaper
interview: 'Soon we may have no more history to document.
The restrictions on crabbing and the closure of the school
represent the death of our community . . . In the next few
years, we will lose even more of the islanders and others will
come in from outside to buy homes here. They're real friendly
but they don't understand our society. They don't understand
our ways.'

We were sitting smack bang opposite the front entrance to
Rukes' Seafood Deck – an establishment that has been cooking
up crabs for a century or more. Our conversation was
punctuated by greetings as every man, woman, boy or girl
passing by offered Jennings a bright 'hello!'

Jennings cleared his throat, and then the lecture began . . .

'To be able to give you a decent history, as I call it, you've
got to go back to the beginning. 'Course, you know the Indians
were the first ones here, back in the fourteenth, fifteenth
century and it might have been earlier – and they spent
hundreds of years using this mostly as an area for hunting,
fishing, whatever. We've got evidence they apparently roasted

their oysters while they were over here and they threw the shells after they'd shucked the oysters. They dug pits and throwed their shells in and so we've got two of those shell middens where they used to dispose of the shells.

''Bout roughly a hundred years later the white man started coming up, you know, and making advances and a group landed at Jamestown about 1607 – John Smith was one of them – he was put in the brig the first time, ha! ha! right after he got here – they resented the fact that he was trying to be an authority within the colony.'

John Smith was born to be in authority, hero material through and through. It was the historian Howard Mumford Jones, who summed up the man's rich life, shot through with energy and adventure: 'He trained himself for knight-errantry, warred against the Mohammedans, put three Turks' heads on his coat-of-arms, was sufficiently a lover to attract the amorous interest of a lady in Constantinople, was a discoverer, a horseman, a navigator, a statesman, a general and a scholar . . . trained in Renaissance ideals.'

Smith's early days in America were difficult, to say the least. He was charged with mutiny and a set of gallows was erected for his judicial murder, but as Jennings explained: 'after a while a daring-do man will find a way, so he got in with the powers that be there, and got the authority to go up the Bay and see if he could discover some precious minerals such as gold and silver. They knew there was a big bay out there but nobody'd ever been in it – they didn't know which direction it was going. I should mention they were in dire need of salt over at Jamestown and they would go over to the Eastern shore of Virginia and see this salt – the tide would come in and when it would go out they would see this salt round the shorelines and they started collecting that – I think they even found a way to strain some water out. I'm not an expert on that.

'Anyway they saw this bay might be of value to the colony and they let John Smith sail up it with about eighteen men, including his physician Walter Russell, so on the first voyage he came on up, he was holding about a north- northwest

19

course and this took him over toward the Eastern shore, not to the shore of Virginia, but it took him over to a place now called Tangier Sound, and to his left or on his port side he saw this chain of islands running up there, and some of them were closer together at that time than they are now. He saw one, then another, then another, and when he got up to about the fourth one a big storm hit him and blew him over to the eastern side of the mainland there. He observed Indians raking in oysters with wooden oyster rakes and he made a note of everything that he saw – he put it in his ship's log. When a storm had come he would write that down. When he observed Indians he would write that down.'

John Smith's descriptions of the native Americans are gloriously vivid, with perhaps more than a generous dash of exaggeration. They were 'couered with the skinnes of wild beasts,' wearing 'large mantels of deare skins not differing much in fashion from the Irish mantels', and they would adorn themselves with 'a dead Rat tied by the tail' or 'with live snakes that often times familiarly would kiss their lips.'

That was just a chance for Jennings to catch his breath. He resumed the tale of Smith's salty quest: 'He was still looking for precious minerals. He didn't hit those, but he did discover a lot of other valuable things. Anyway he went past this chain, past these islands and he saw a couple more, but he was still not in the Bay proper, he was over in what we call now the tributaries – going up to the Eastern shore. As he worked his way up, he hit a straits up there – it's now known as Hooper Straits but he recorded the Straits of Limbo, meaning, I guess, it was kind of tedious getting through these channels. I think they ran ashore on several occasions on that voyage.

'On one trip, after he'd been up as far as he could go, he started making his trip back to the Rappahannock river. He was a restless guy; he wanted to be active all the time, so while he was waiting for the barge to float he went over on the flats, and some of these fish and crabs were trapped on this extreme low tide. He was just walking on the flats with his sword – nonchalantly sticking it in stingrays' backs and flipping them over his shoulder, but one apparently didn't flip and the tail stuck in his wrist. They're poisonous – the dorsal spines on the tail – and he became deathly ill and he thought he was going to die. His eyesight started failing and he told them to set him up on the bank where he could look at the Bay as if that was going to be his last glance – he wanted some good scenery to go out by – but anyway his doctor, Walter Russell, happened to have salve aboard the boat and he went and saturated the wound. Just a little while later Smith started feeling better and he decided he wasn't going to die, so later that evening, according to his log, he had the same fish for dinner but that might be a fishy story! That was his first trip up, and as a result of his doctor's good deed in saving his life he named those chain of islands that he first come across the Russell Isles.

'Smith made another voyage – this time he went out in the Bay proper. As far as this area is concerned, he charted all these islands and named them the Russell Isles. Fifty years later, another Englishman, Henry Smith, was responsible for bringing twenty new subjects from England – it was his beckoning to the New World that brought them. It wasn't an easy life and not everybody wanted to come, and once they got here it was the custom in those days in Jamestown that the governor Berkeley rewarded people like that who brought others in, so apparently he awarded him an island in Chesapeake Bay, this in about 1665, something like that.

'Now, he thought he was in Maryland, and when he made his way up the Eastern shore he found a residence in Accommack County – some of the people that were coming from Jamestown – some of them were being persecuted just like they were in England – when they got to Jamestown some of these people wanted them all to belong to the Church of England – and they had others branching out as Quakers and different little sects and this rubbed them up the wrong way. They were being persecuted here just like where they ran away from. Anyway the Quakers moved on up and other little sects moved on up – some of them because they wanted to roam –

see what this new land was all about – you always get a few adventurers in any colony.'

The names of the early settlements speak volumes about the demands and challenges of pioneering life back then – Hunger River, World's End Creek which runs out of Hell Hook Marsh, Men's Burial Point, Devil's Island – which was to mutate into Deal's Island – Rumbling Point, Damned Quarter, Tedious Creek and the fabulously named Transquaking River.

So, back to Jennings and Henry Smith. 'Smith came on up to the Eastern shore and stayed awhile and then he met another fellow, William Stephens, who had stopped in Virginia on the Eastern shore. He had come a little earlier and had come to know the Maryland legislature and the way it operated. He was what they'd call a land entrepreneur – in other words, he had authority from Lord Baltimore to dispense big tracts of land to people coming up from Jamestown, and they were kind of streaming up, some of them for persecution's sake some others 'cause they wanted to find a new area. The Lord Baltimore at the time was offering fifty acres of land to each one of them to come up, if they'd settle near the boundary line of Maryland and Virginia. Once Stephens and Smith met, they became good friends and actually the biggest county that was in that area at that time, they helped organise it. Well, Stephens had a tract of land over on Smith Island, so did Smith who had the southern part surrounded by the Governor of Jamestown. Stephens already had a part granted from Lord Baltimore – it was the northern part of the island. Stephens conveyed his thousand acres to go with Smith's island land. It wasn't called Smith Island then, it was just called 'an island.' But when he got it it, was called Smith – it was called the Captain Henry Smith estate – not because he was a big sea captain but because he was a captain in the militia over in Somerset County – one of the biggest counties in the new colony of Maryland.

Stephens later became a representative in Lord Baltimore's general assembly. Smith also became a representative and they sort of ran the county, but Smith's undoing was that he was one of those kind who would get rich for a while and then he'd kind of lose his money and he was kind of a philanderer too. His first wife, Joanne, sued him in court and divorced him and got a big bundle even in those days. The man had means and couldn't get along with his wife – the wife sort of made it payback time. After that Smith didn't spend a lot of time here – he would commute backwards and fores to the mainland – only on business trips mostly – there's no record that he lived here steady – although they said that he had one of his women over here – he commuted back and fore occasionally to see her. He got depleted of funds again and started selling off parcels of his island and by that time the regular settlers started coming up – the permanent settlers. There were settlers here from St. Mary's before, conducting samples of soil to see what could be grown here – one guy thought it would be a good place to raise cattle – a man called Robert Kedge. Apparently it worked because the last cattle didn't leave that area until 1948.

'Let's get back to Smith. John Evans came from the mainland of Virginia. His father had migrated through Jamestown about 1656 – we don't know the exact date because there's a lot more John Evanses came through within a thirteen-year period and it's hard to pinpoint which one; he stayed to a place called Silver Thorn Ridge – it's no longer there but some two mile below the present town of Bloxxom, Virginia.

'His older son John married a girl in that community, Elizabeth Ewell. He knew a lot of people on the mainland who wanted to come over to the island to see what could be done over there. They were adventurous – no doubt because they knew they were going to suffer – they had to come by boat and I'm sure there were more insects then than there are now, but anyway he made up his mind to come on over here, and apparently he'd met Henry Smith on the mainland and had agreed to buy 200 acres of his northern part of the part that William Stephens had once owned. Just about the same time John Tyler, another Englishman, came and bought a piece of the southern part, 200 acres for 9000 pounds of tobacco. See, they used tobacco for money in those days – when they made a transaction Smith began to regain a little bit of income, or a part of his lost fortune.

'That's when it began: all the present-day settlers belong to either the Evanses or Tylers or both – most are related to both.

'The Bradshaws came in the 1700s and settled on Holland Island – which sank really. Now there's just enough left there really to support a few cemeteries and some of those are washing. In the late 1800s they had a terrific hurricane, and right after it they had evidence of the land just washing away, it was like it was dropping off in chunks. Later on, in 1920, all 320 people had to be evacuated.'

The last Holland islander left in 1922 and his house became the home of the Holland Island Gun Club. It was a busy, established community with a congregation of sixty homes, a church, a two-room schoolhouse and a post office. All now claimed by the voracious waves.

Jennings settled into talk of demography. 'We had about 100 in 1800, fifty per cent of them Evanses, about twenty-five per cent was Tylers and then you had the Bradshaws coming into Holland Island and settling.

'As time went on, they farmed areas – the dream was to find a good high piece of land known as a hammock – a farm place really – where they could grow fruit trees in orchards and other crops and feed their cattle. They fished but that weren't their daily bread – they were just like the mainland. They even tried to raise tobacco and cotton, watermelons and sweet potatoes . We'd still do that if we had enough land – the soil's certainly rich enough – but what happened, the salt started encroaching, and it wasn't conducive to growing anything. They wanted to get near a harbour where they could get their vessels and they wanted a marsh close by – it weren't no accident – because in the wintertime they could get their musket out and go out there and there's wildfowl and all that. That's all they did – feed 'erselves and clothe 'erselves and I guess every blue moon a ship would come in from England and they might get some store-bought items. No doubt they could catch crabs and oysters and fish.

24

'I'm not so sure about crabs. I can't remember even back in my time where people ate a lot of crabs like they do now – that's just come on the last forty years – people going crazy over steam crab. I remember they used to stew some and put them in a pot and gravy and onions and dumplings, and I swear they were good – if you could just keep the things from slipping out your hand! No doubt in the eighteen hundreds they used some seafood to supplement their diet.

'This went on, just little families scattered at random around the Bay, but they would still use little boats to go through the guts that intertwine through the whole island – the island's about nine miles long and four miles wide and it might have been even wider than that in those days. I do know they had farms which extended out much further but they're now washed away.

'That was the beginning of the problem – when the Bay started washing day in, day out – storms and all – washing a little bit here and a little bit there and first thing you know after a period of years the rate of erosion picks up. In 1872 they were making a deposition with the authorities of Virginia and Maryland trying to establish where this new state line was to go and we the old people, our descendants – thought it should stay right where it was anyway. We think it was the people living below the line who really had the influence on moving that line up. When George Washington was in office, the line was just right – it started from the lower shore of the Potomac river and it ran straight to the southern end of Pocomoke sound, which give the Tangier Island and Smith's Island watermen an equal amount of oystering area. Farming went on until 1840. Laben Evans, he had farmed all his life – born about 1783 and died about 1850 – probably he never did work on the water, but he had seven sons plus a lot of daughters and he had all this – right where we are now. It was right for one man, but the reason I make a note of him is because this is the point from where they start to become watermen.

'He had seven sons; well, he tried to share his land with them – to divide up the parcels and by that time they'd heard

25

that these New Englanders had come down from Connecticut and Long Island Sound and they were out there dredging these oysters out in Chesapeake Bay. Well, Maryland and Virginia watermen hadn't been doing it commercially – they probably couldn't get anything for them if they did. They put them on guard that it might be a way to make a few pennies here, being the farmland was washing away and what they did to make the New Englanders stop oystering, they concocted a residency law – you had to be born in either of these States – or you can't just go out and take the oysters anywhere you want.

'That still didn't deter 'em – they sent buy boats down – they were regular schooners – to buy from the Maryland and Virginia watermen for ten cents a bushel. They could get their schoonerload and still go back legally, so another thing they did – they were used to shucking oysters and all in New England – well some of them come down and opened up oyster houses in Baltimore and Crisfield and all and got in on the oyster boom, because this Bay was full of oysters at that time, about 1850s.

'The sons of Laben Evans got some schooners a bit before that. They had a whole fleet, and they started drawing people from the mainland to man these boats – there weren't that many people here. That was the end of the farming as we knew it. By 1900 everybody was registered either as oysterman or a fisherman because the land was just washing away and wouldn't bear farming. Each one of these fellas had a little garden, you know, to supplement their diet with vegetables. They didn't get rich – they caught fifteen million bushels but they were only bringing ten to fifteen cents a bushel so they caught a lot of oysters but didn't get wealthy at it. Now the Civil War started about 1861 and some of the areas were closed down and they couldn't make a living oystering.

'They needed more men to man the schooners – they had eight to ten crew and used to wind their dredges by hand. Seven black families settled on the island. New names were heard – Middletons, Corbins, Sommers – and the population shot up. By 1910 it was the highest it got – 805 people. By 1947 we were down to 750. With the First World War the people began to slide – some went to work in defence plants – all of Rhodes Point pretty much left.

'With the land washing away many people moved, some to Crisfield and others to Ewell. One family put their whole house on a barge and floated it across. What happened then gave us names we use now. Drum Point was so called because they caught a lot of drum fish in the 1700s. Ewell was named after Oscar B. Ewell – the postmaster in Crisfield – who was also a surgeon at the hospital – who named it in 1885. Tylerton – most of the families came from there. They also created cemeteries here. They were here seventy years before the churches.'

Jennings then went on to explain the origins of his burning and abiding interest in history. 'When I was little, we didn't have much time for genealogy – crabbers don't have time to go crawling through graveyards. That's how Rhodes Point began really – as a graveyard. A fella called King Richard Evans, who was a great-grandson of John Evans, he brought his wife to Rhodes Point. That was a cemetery before it was ever a community.'

The water was Jennings' world in those days.

'I used to get out on the bow of the skiff a'crabbing with a net, looking for peelers, that's what they used to do – you see a crab and you real quick get it – you need quick reflexes and a good balance to keep from falling overboard. I got to wondering – I'd look at all these old sites and these old bluffs and trees and these hammocks and I'd say, I wonder who was the first guy on this island? I just left it up to my little mind to figure out. I bet my grandfather No-ee – we can't say Noah it's too hard on out lips; we say No-ee – No-ee Tobe was the first man. I didn't realise there were about six generations ahead of him. My grandfather's father was buried to his homestead right near the Bay.

'My father was born over on the western side of the Bay. He didn't live where we are now until 1920. His father had a home right by the Bay and they were being encroached on too. His father was a farmer and a waterman – he found it necessary to get his boat out and catch a few oysters. The change came quickly. In 1840 there were sixty-nine farmers on Smith. By the turn of the century the waves had eaten at the land and made it salty, so the crops – the corn, the sweet potatoes, tobacco and tomatoes stopped growing. By 1900 there wasn't one farmer.

'My father went to Baltimore during the war to work on the Liberty ships – three hundred and eighty four ships left that one shipyard, taking supplies to England and Russia, the factories going full blast. When we came back I missed the electricity appliances in Baltimore. Until poles went up, in 1947, we just had lamps. They'd light up a room dimly.

'Crabs would leave with both World Wars. I remember this man, he invented this crab pot – a square wire box and he put a piece of bait in the centre – where the crabs could avoid each other.'

Jennings worked on water when he was twenty, and spent a further forty-five years harvesting the Bay. The army took him overseas. After basic training in El Paso he then spent two years overseas in Korea.

Having spent a long afternoon listening to his extempore lecture, buoyed up on swelling waves of enthusiasm for his subject, I realised that here was a man who, given the breaks, could have been a sterling academic, or, gauging by his popularity round the place, run for governor.

Later that day I went with thirteen-year-old Craig Evans from Ewell to Tylerton. We went through the creeks, and as we drew closer to Tylerton the little boat went through the marsh's equivalent to a ghost town, deserted shanties, tattered buildings tottering on spindly legs. As he steered the craft Craig chatted brightly.

'Getting to school involves getting up real early – it's an eight-hour day, another hour to get home. I hope to work the water, not that I'd like to spend my life doing it.' His father owns the Janet Lynn, a thirty-foot boat, and had about four hundred pots in the water, which is more than average.

So what are the attractions of working the water? 'The pleasures of working the water are a lot of hard work. If you do good you get paid real good.'

But there are problems. 'Crab regulation – people saying crabs are scarce – they say that and everyone goes into an immediate panic, but no one over here cares as long as we catches some crabs. I mean catching crabs ain't no scarce around here. Everybody around here just about works on the water – just about all the men work on the water and the women shuck crabs.'

'I trap muskrats to get the skin; didn't catch many this year but I didn't go so far. I set the traps near the trails they use. The money varies – might get good money for it if people want fur coats.' Muskrats are the most abundant aquatic mammals in the Chesapeake, ten to sixteen inches long, with seven-inch, scaly and hairless tails. You need an awful lot to make a coat.

Craig is phlegmatic – a little resigned to the fate of the island. 'By the time I'm forty it could be all gone. I mean the Corps of Engineers redid the part that was affected the most – they used some canvas-type material – they dredged up where it's shallow and pumped it into there. When they came here it helped in two ways – it made the water deeper and it packed up some land. In two or three hundred years it could be all gone.'

Chapter 4

UNDERWATER DISCOTHEQUE

Top predator and reliable canary, the waterman would certainly seem worth keeping around, a fitting symbol of the kind of Bay we want to preserve.

Tom Horton, *Bay Country*

There are only two weeks in the year when the watermen can depend on naked sex. Among the crabs that is. For two weeks in May a male crab called a Jimmie, set as a sex-lure within a pot, will be sufficiently enticing a presence to attract a host of fecund females, or snooks, as handmaidens to his court. Set two Jimmies, and there are enough pheromones, or whatever agent attracts the ladies, to cause a near riot down there among the weeds. Down there they dance a muddy meringue, an underwater tango.

The Latin name of the Atlantic blue crab, *Callinectes sapidus*, means 'beautiful and savoury swimmer'. In the Chesapeake they swim in their millions. Mary Rathbun, who gave the crab this name – among a thousand other species which she named during her lifetime – was the doyenne of American carcinology, but the blue crab's scientific name is the only one she created which mixes gastronomy with taxonomy.

The harvest of beautiful and savoury swimmers is the fourth most important fishery in America – after shrimp, salmon and tuna – making the United States the largest consumer of crabs in the world, with the Japanese licking their lips in second place. The blue crab makes up half the USA catch, alongside other species such as the Alaskan king crab, the Dungeness crab of the Pacific coast, the Alaskan snow crab, the Florida stone crab and Maine's Jonah and rock crabs.

Blue crabs are the bedrock of the Smith Island economy. The crabs may have an extensive biological range that sweeps grandly from Long Island to Texas but the underwater meadows made up of the great swathes of sea grass that surround Smith have the greatest concentrations, a veritable cornucopia of crabs. Millions of tons of crabs are harvested annually in the Chesapeake and have a tasty reputation. Served on the best platters in the big cities they are enough to make a gastronome quiver with expectation.

It was still dark when I joined Carl Tyler and Chris Parkes as they readied their boat for a day on the Bay. Their shanty sits just across the way from Carl's home. Carl Tyler is forty-seven years of age and started crabbing when he was seven years old. In those early days his father would pay him the princely sum of a dollar a day which he had to put in the bank. Carl's son Robbie has followed his father onto the water. Robbie's just twenty-two years old, but he already has his own boat and is just about to get married to a woman from Rhodes Point – another Tyler from another branch of the family – but as Carl opines, 'if you go back we're all the same.' His other son, William, is about to graduate from high school and wants to join the Marines.

Chris, who is helping him out during this busy period, is a journalist and a graduate of philosophy. The routines of crabbing can be mind-numbing, and the emptiness of the Bay can challenge thought itself. So Chris silently considers Spinoza as he responds to the rhythm of the work. Carl, similarly, is a keen reader, though not of philosophy. Appropriately for a waterman, he was reading Dana Sobel's *Longitude* at home at the time of my stay in Chesapeake Bay.

Carl comes from a long line of watermen. 'My father was a waterman, a skipjack captain, as was my grandfather and my great-grandfather and my great-great-grandfather.'

Carl and I discussed the authorship of Shakespeare's plays as we headed out to open water, crossing the Chesapeake toward Point Lookout, Maryland. It was strange when the ghosts of Christopher Marlowe and William Shakespeare seemingly

31

joined us in the cabin to claim their quills. Carl loves Shakespeare. 'That's something I like to read. I get a lot of lessons out of it, especially *Macbeth* – I think the lesson in that play is don't get too greedy for power and money, and I remember his lament: "Tomorrow, and tomorrow, and tomorrow/Creeps in this petty pace from day to day/to the last syllable of recorded time;/and all our yesterdays have lighted fools/the way to dusty death." For me that's the most important part of that whole play.'

Carl loves the histories as well as the tragedies. He particularly enjoys *Henry V*, especially the chorus's evocation of the two armies, bedded down – 'he can describe that so good.'

> *Now entertain conjecture of a time*
> *When creeping murmur and the poring dark*
> *Fills the wide vessel of the universe.*
> *From camp to camp, through the foul womb of the night,*
> *The hum of either army stilly sounds . . .*

Shakespeare has been a part of the island's culture ever since a man called King Solomon began the first school in the 1790s where the plays were studied along with the Bible, Pilgrim's Progress and a hymn book.

Our talk of literature was accompanied by the thrum of the boat's engines – so much like the hum of two armies lying with breath bated and expectancy running through them like a taut wire – and put me in mind of a quote by the late Gilbert Byron, the Chesapeake poet, who once described the watermen as 'the greatest poets/who never wrote a line.' They have an elemental and poetic relationship with nature and, although they are avowedly Methodist, there is nothing fanciful whatsoever about seeing them as being in some ways pantheists, seeing God through nature, the bestower of abundant harvests in the waters, the bringer of millpond calm waters after punishing winds – known as 'nosers' by the islanders – God as the opener of dawn's gates and author of sunset's closing act. Elemental is a good word to use hereabouts – the waters of the Bay carry, in solution, every natural element present in the periodic table.

We headed out to open water as the sun rose – a silk swirl of red and darker. Veins of bloodshot purple leached colour into the insipid grey sky overhead as Carl set a course for the mouth of the Potomac river. This is where he had set his crab pots – twenty-five rows, ten pots to a row – planted in the waves much as a potato farmer sets his plants in trenches, to be harvested later on.

A ghost ship loomed up out of the darkness, its metal hull rendered insubstantial by wraiths of mist. It was the *American Mariner*, one of the fleet of Liberty ships built on Roosevelt's orders by America during the Second World War. At the time it was estimated that U-boats were sinking transports at twice the rate that they could be built by the British and USA shipyards combined. They were built as disposable vessels, with a life expectancy of five years. Hundreds of ships were to stretch across the Atlantic in convoys, which formed, to quote the President, a 'bridge of ships'. The *Mariner* is still a target, used by the air force jets that scream over from nearby Bloodworth Island to plant their bombs and missiles.

The chatter of the watermen on the VHF radios was constant and excitable. A man called Peewee enthused about the trip he'd made the previous evening up to Atlantic City for a touch of heavy metal at a Van Halen concert. Carl replied that he wouldn't cross the road to see Van Halen perform. Carl is a trifle more conservative in his taste in music. He likes *Riverdance* which he saw on PBS, syncopated stepping-out with a vengeance. The heavy metal afficionado offered Carl a bit of homespun philosophy – 'Long day come too quick' he said, and you could almost hear a touch of weariness through the white noise and static. As he steered a course for the next line of pots, munching the first of his snack breakfasts, Carl told me about the warm generosity of watermen.

Swiftly disposing of a slab of chocolate cake – seven-layer chocolate cake is one of the island specialities – he told me a tale about a waterman who was fishing off Deal island when his crab pot wrapped itself around the cooler pipes, sinking the boat in fifty foot of water. His dog drowned and the poor man was left with no visible means of support, so the watermen held a Telethon on the radio and raised $70,000. To cap it all, a man from Cambridge *gave* him a boat.

A huge barge, as big as a city block, loomed up. The *Orient Trader* was carrying 120 freight containers, maybe bound for Baltimore. We passed a lighthouse, prompting Carl to tell me that his great-great-great-great-grandfather was a lighthouse keeper. A tug towing a barge followed in the wake of the *Trader*, heading for Salisbury or Cambridge.

Chris pointed out that his degree in philosophy 'along with seventy-nine cents, will get you a cup of coffee in Dunkin' Donuts.' He is keen on Existentialism, Sartre, Camus, Buddhism and Daoism. Some of Chris's ancestors lived on the state line – one was a bootlegger selling to Virginia. His significant other, Shelley Hitchens, is an artist from Baltimore. She painted the big map that greets visitors to Tylerton.

The two watermen donned overtrousers and heavy-duty Neoprene gloves. They need to be heavy-duty: gloves may only last two weeks during busy periods. Carl navigated the boat to the beginning of the line of pots. The pots are emptied out onto a large stainless steel tray and the catch is sorted. This pot brought with it a great many things other than crabs – a thrashing of eels and a slithering of early sea nettles, glutinous white jellyfish which can cause real pain should a shrapnel-blob get in one's eye. The traditional way to deal with the sting is to apply baking soda.

The eels reminded me of one of those facts garnered from one of Rachel Carson's wonderful accounts of the sea. It bears repeating, as it is compelling proof of nature's ability to humble and amaze. The eel can recognise some scents even when diluted to three parts per quintillion, equivalent to adding an ounce of aroma to the whole of the Chesapeake. Perhaps this goes some way to explaining the migratory feat of the eel in making its way to the Sargasso Sea – the saltiest part of the Atlantic, which, in turn, is the saltiest of the world's

34

oceans. It perhaps smells its way to the saltiness of this marine zone, for zone it is. Draw a line from the Chesapeake to Gibraltar and that would be its northern edge, another line connecting Haiti with Dakar on the west coast of Africa would be its southerly perimeter. And it is big, as big as the United States, and extends halfway across the Atlantic. This eel on the deck before me, snaking and sliding, wriggling and writhing, was a mighty explorer. It had been to a sea forgotten by winds, a place filled with sailors' memories of the treacherous Bermuda Triangle. It coiled and uncoiled in a corner and waited for the push of a long-handled brush to cast it back into the waters.

The caught crabs shone green, blue and orange scarlet. Some frothed at the gills. Crabs that had shed a few days previously were ignominiously tossed back into the water.

The shore hereabouts was studded with houses that reminded one of Russian dachas, desirable shoreline residences set among ridges of pine trees. We passed the site of Camp Hoffman, which housed a huge number of prisoners of war during the Civil War. Here the constant arc-lamp glare of the light coming off water was enough to blind some of the prisoners. Sanitation was poor, and the camp was open to all weathers. With anything up to 10,000 men incarcerated at any one time, Hoffman was hellish. Carl informed me that some of the people on Smith Island descended from escapees from the camp – the very lucky ones. It makes for hardy stock, a historical backbone set in place.

As if prompted by the tale, Carl donned a pair of shades that wouldn't look out of place on Park Avenue. Chris was meanwhile pondering the fact that in the East they eat all manner of insects while 'in the West we don't, yet we eat crabs and snails . . .' We then caught an oyster toad fish, perfectly described by Mark E. Jacoby in his book, *Working the Chesapeake: Watermen on the Bay*, as 'an ugly, barbeled, loose-jowled and fat-headed fish that preys upon young oysters, crushing them in its massive jaws.'

Carl told me how NASA sent an oyster toad into space to

conduct neurological experiments on the effects of weightlessness. 'All the watermen thought it was a big joke.' Three or four of the watermen fish specifically for oyster toads, as they are fish with no backbones or bones. It is a curious species. The male makes a den using shells, and sounds a foghornlike call to females who lay their eggs upside down on the roof of the den, where the male fertilises them and then guards the young oyster toads as they grow.

A loon, or great northern diver, resplendent in its telephone-black and whiter-than-white plumage flies past. This might have been a bird of passage. Able to dive up to 150 feet, loons are wildly adept at chasing fish. The loon is followed by a pelican that seems to have the aerodynamic shape of a cargo plane.

Some crabs were already dead when they were brought up out of the water. These were kept together in a tray of dead crabs for dumping in deeper water – watermen believe that crab cadavers scare off the living ones.

The sun was climbing inexorably upwards towards its noonday zenith and its rays, reflected off the white paintwork of the boat, felt as if they were coming off a blowtorch. 'There are days when it gets a bit mirey out here,' Carl told me, 'but today is certainly not one of those.' It certainly wasn't. You could have fried an egg on the cabin roof.

By now we had crossed right across the Bay to just above Point Lookout. This was unusual for Carl – most of his crabbing is done on the eastern side of the Chesapeake. He works long hours, Stakhanovite labour indeed: 'It varies right now,' he says, 'it's more than at any other time during the season.' He usually clocks up ten to twelve hours every day as they try to capitalise on the runs of crabs.

'Crabs have different cycles that they go through, and it's the moulting of 'em, and they shed and then they become hard crabs again, and then after that they'll do the process all over again until they get to the size that they won't do it any more, and each one of those cycles is like a run we call it. The biggest run is in the springtime because in the wintertime they're dormant – they don't go through that process; they do it more during this time of year than at any other time during the season and all the other runs that we have will be smaller. We crab from the first of April until the end of November and then if the oyster season looks good we'll do that until mid March.'

Crab pots came late to the Chesapeake. They were first designed in Virginia in the 1930s although aquatic traps themselves date back to the very beginning of recorded time. The father of history, Herodotus, visited the people who lived on the edge of Lake Prasias, where fish were so plentiful that 'a man has only to open his trap door, and let down a basket by a rope into the water, and then wait a very short time, when he draws it up quite full of fish.' Plato, in a prayer for a young man, urged that 'no desire of hunting in the sea, or of catching the creatures in the waters ever take possession of you, either when you are awake, or when you are asleep, by hooks, with weels, which latter is a very lazy contrivance – a weel being a willow eel pot.' Many materials have historically been used to make traps, from the wicker used to contain a mess of eels, to ceramic pots for octopuses, lath pots for crabs, fish and lobsters and wire pots which imprison unsuspecting Chesapeake blues.

Chris explained what he's looking for. 'Right here on the back fin you see a pink band of colour – "the pink sign" – which means it's rank and ready to moult. This should shed – become a soft crab – in forty-eight to seventy-two hours. Sexing crabs is easy – all females "paint their fingernails" – that is they have bright red tips to their claws.' These here are the male crabs – the Jimmies. Peelers are about to "peel" their outer shell. The paperthin new shell is easy to eat, a delicacy for diners which doesn't involve the hard graft of picking sweet white meat from a very hard shell.'

The lexicon of crabs is complicated – there are fifty words for crab – rivalling the Innuit with their many names for snow, the Arabs with their rich vocabulary for camels or the Australian aboriginal's host of words to describe different kinds of holes. A *keeper* is a crab big enough to keep, usually around five inches. Anything less is prohibited by Maryland law. *Busters* are crabs emerging from old shells. *Softshells* are the emergent crabs. *Papershell* crabs have shells that have stiffened a little. *Buckram* crabs are papershells where the shell is beginning to harden but still remains pliable. *Hardshells* have, as their name suggests, hardened shells, usually about four days after shedding. Egg-heavy females – which cannot be harvested, thus protecting future harvests – are variously known as *sponges, lemon bellies, ballies, busted sooks* and *punks.* Medium-sized crabs are *hotels* or simply *mediums,* while bigger creatures are known as *whales* or *jumbos. Doublers,* also known as *bucks and riders,* are male and female crabs caught in *flagrante delicto* moving as a unit, male above and female below.

The last pot was hauled on board dripping all the way. 'It's kind of a typical morning for the end of the run,' said Carl. 'We'll take it home now and put them in the floats – a sort of wide bathtub more or less – with water going into them all the time, and we'll dump our catch in that. Then follows the process of shedding the crabs, meaning that they moult, come out, become soft crabs and then we get them out of the tanks then pack 'em up and send them to Crisfield.'

Carl believes with all sincerity that the crabs are given as acts of Providence: 'As far back as I can remember the water business has been unpredictable and you have to put your faith in something. The people round here put their faith in God most of the time and we think if we're good people He'll bless us with a good catch.'

There are more and more days now when his faith is put to the test, but as he says phlegmatically, 'It seems like that's always the way and something always comes up.'

For most of his working life Carl has worked the water alone. Only during the past eight to ten years has he carried anyone with him. He is glad that his son Robbie has followed him to work the crabbing grounds. He is proud of the young man's skills: 'He's a pretty good waterman for his age,' he says. 'Not that I want him to mirror everything I do. I like to let them think for their ownselves – things like where to put the pots and how to make things a little easier on yourself.'

38

Using Jimmies to entice females into the pot is a trick which lasts no more than two weeks. At other times different techniques are used to tempt crabs into the wire enclosures, which Carl enumerated to me. 'Peeler potting, for instance, involves throwing the pots in with nothing in them and the peeler crab tries to find a place to shed – they like a dark closed place and they'll go in there thinking it's a safe place to hide and that's called peeler potting. There's another kind which is called hard crab potting where the only way you can get the crabs in there is to put some sort of bait in there – like alewives or herring, sometimes mackerel, and they go in there to eat the bait.

'Crabbing ends on November thirtieth when Maryland tells us we have to quit. For two or three years they made us quit on the fifteenth. We had to take up the pots when we were still catching crabs and making money. We didn't like that too much.'

Carl sees the bureaucrats as a hindrance. 'They want to get rid of the small feeder. Virginia used to be pretty liberal with their catch laws but now it seems they're doing a lot to hinder us from crabbing there, like the pot on the bottom there to cover up the little pot in a pot – we call it the feed pot. It was once used to put bait in. Now they want to cover that up to keep the small crabs out, but they will still get in and shed, and they want you to put rings in them, supposedly to let out these smaller crabs, but the real reason is that they want to put obstacles in our way. Then another thing they've done is to put an exorbitant amount of money on their licence fees. If I go into Virginia – I had my licence there one time – it cost $500, but now that I've given that up I can't go back down there, I have to be on a waiting list to get a licence so just anybody can't go there.'

Enforcing these laws in Maryland is the job of the Natural Resources Police. 'Occasionally they will come round to your boat. They'll meet you at the place where you take crabs out and they'll look them over.' Some watermen have become policemen – poachers turned gamekeepers, some might say.

'I used to do telephone work around here, but we lost that job through the union. I kind of miss that check. I worked in the correctional facility and I tried to do this too. I didn't know what stress was until that job.'

So despite the backbreaking labour and punishing hours, Carl enjoys being a waterman. 'It's enormous freedom for me. I get up at the time I want. I'm not answerable to anybody and I live on an island where family is important. It's one of the things I like about it. Take Chris there. I knew his dad, I knew his mother, I knew his mother's dad and I know his sisters and I know his brother. Anybody walking down the street I can tell who their mother was and their father was, and there are very few places you can do that nowadays, very few places.'

The day's work is punctuated by visits to the tanks – three times a day – at five o'clock, noon and six in the evening. They take the soft crabs 'and put them in the cooler at about forty-eight degrees – that way they don't harden up anymore.' They use seagrass to pack them, especially if they're going to New York's Fulton fish market or they use the sort of bubble wrap one uses for wrapping delicate or precious objects.

All this is achieved through fairly hefty investment. 'A shanty will set you back some seventeen to twenty thousand dollars, a boat would cost you between thirty-five and fifty thousand dollars, and of the order of fifteen thousand dollars for the necesssary crab pots . . .'

They can charge ten dollars apiece for crabs on the dining tables of Boston. The mark-up between crabber and diner is considerable and the middlemen, as in so many fields of enterprise, are not slow to make a fast buck. Carl shrugged his shoulders: he is a born stoic. 'I get a decent price I guess.'

The same stoicism was evident in Chris's voice as he considered the changes that have been rung on Smith. 'Smith Island is a vanishing culture, mostly because the outside world seems to have discovered it, and we've continued to discover the outside world and our values are getting more in line with America in general. Most people seem to own a television, so that the official flower around here is the satellite dish. We see the same television programming as the mainland, we shop at the same stores. Culture's getting homogenous – we all eat at MacDonalds, we all buy our goods at Walmart. One of the most celebrated facets of America is the small town. But small towns don't seem any different any more.'

Chris also aired his anxieties about the health of the Bay. 'The Bay is under enormous pressure from population growth and some overfishing – right now there's fifteen million people living on the Bay. In ten years there will be eighteen million. I don't think the Bay can handle that, really. I don't think it's realistic to expect the Bay to stay in any kind of decent shape ecologically as long as you've got that many people pouring things into it.

'For every waterman there's a hundred thousand voters out there in the Bay watershed and it's pretty obvious that things are not going well with the Bay so we do become a sort of convenient whipping boy. I would say we contribute in a small way to the problem of the Bay, but the real problems seem to be the people who do vote and do join the environmental movement – they seem to think that the fifty dollars they contribute to organisations like the Bay Foundation is a means of fighting pollution but the real way to fight pollution is to change our behaviour – don't fertilise your front lawn, buy a car that gets forty miles to the gallon – *then* you're saving the Bay.'

The waterman can be seen as a sensitive litmus paper for assessing the health of the Bay. As Tom Horton put it:

> . . . *Of all the human users of the Bay, only the waterman absolutely requires resources of a quantity and variety that presuppose a natural system in top, year-round condition. Put another way, the waterman is to the rest of us Bay dwellers what the canary was to coal miners, who carried them down the shafts, depending on the bird's exquisite sensitivity to leaking gas to give them an early warning of disaster. If watermen are flourishing, it is a sign that the Bay's integrity still holds.*

The Foundation and the Human Canaries have locked horns in the past. 'I know a number of people in the Foundation,'

41

says Chris. 'Their hearts are in the right place; they do want the best for the Bay, but they've become a very large organisation with a goal of being self-sustaining – they have to survive because they have to meet a payroll. They have a lot of people who are depending on them – so they have to take advantage of anything they can to draw attention to themselves, to what they're doing, to seek out contributions both from individuals and more and more from corporations. Whereas the watermen – while they may on one level seem like predators or seem to be doing the Bay harm – really their fate is tied up with the Bay and they're as concerned about it as any environmentalist – if not more so. I don't think any environmentalist will lose his or her job if the pollution gets worse – in fact they'll need *more* environmentalists if the pollution gets worse, whereas there'll be fewer of us. Instead of attacking the general population, which seems to support environmental groups, the Bay Foundation seem to think that there's a political and economic advantage in attacking us, although I think they learned their lesson from the last time. There has been an effort on their part to try and understand the problems and I hope the watermen will make an effort to understand what their problems and goals are.'

The Chesapeake Foundation is, as Chris Points out, a very large organisation boasting 82,000 members, 125 employees, a $7 million budget, seventeen education-research vessels and three mobile canoe fleets. Up to 30,000 children take to the water under their aegis, to study and enjoy the Chesapeake's many and myriad glories. The Foundation is very big, and certainly an effective lobby group, but . . . it does have a big payroll.

The island is washing away, the sea level is rising, right here on the wharf where Carl ties his boat. 'I used to work on this wharf a long time ago with my father and we hardly ever experienced high tide,' he says. So far this spring I've seen water covering the roads thirty per cent of the time and that is extremely unusual, so I think the evidence is there. If it was just the roads I might say the roads are settling, but it's also coming up over the wharf.'

Chris likes certain aspects of working on the water, but his ambitions are necessarily limited. 'I don't have my own boat. I have to work for other people and the investment to get started in this business or running your own boat is so high that I'm very reluctant to invest so much money in something that I'm not sure of anymore. Twenty years ago it was cheaper and I was more optimistic, but I chose to go away to college. I don't regret that decision, but sometimes I wish I'd made more of an effort to make a life here for myself. I expect we'll be leaving and I will miss it.'

Chris feels isolated as a philosophy graduate. 'On an intellectual level I do but on a community level, no! I feel a part of it. These are good people and even though we may have differences about this and that, I like just about everybody here. I trust them: they know me, I know them, we get along just fine. I don't have a real problem with anybody here.

'Here there's a sense of community, of belonging to something larger than yourself, a sense of neighbourliness, of family, and of extended family. And once you know people as well as we know each other it's hard not to look after everybody and that's very rare. There's a song by Billy Joel which has a line about there being no island left for islanders like me – more and more there are outsiders moving in and there's a different atmosphere and, here on the Eastern shore we are living economically in a backwater. I found that I couldn't trust people in college because I didn't know their families – even though they were nice people, mind.

'There are two images of watermen – a romantic folklore figure involved in brave exploits on the Bay and then there's the surly waterman who can't be trusted to take care of the Bay. There are probably watermen who'll chase the last crab into a corner and kill it, and there are other watermen who'll work every day and are trying to take care of what they know is irreplaceable.

'I think that if the watermen continue to learn to exploit the resources at the same rate that they are right now I wonder if there will be be crab stocks in fifty years, even in thirty years from now. If the people of Annapolis and Richmond and Harrisburg, Pennsylvania will start acting on behalf of the Bay instead of doing what is politically expedient, the future of the Bay will be better than its present course suggests.'

I diplomatically referred to the fact that the good people of Smith tend to be a bit on the large side (speaking as a large man myself). 'Yeah, the people of Smith eat an awful lot of food. The second favourite pastime after watching TV is eating. They have a lot of cholestrol, a lot of fat and lot of sugar. People like to eat here. It's some of the most unhealthy eating you'll ever encounter – margarine, grease, tartar sauce – trouble is it tastes so good. My wife is appalled.' On Smith even the most delicate seafood comes wrapped in a thick exoskeleton of batter. With tartar sauce.

The food provides the energy to work hard, although many people seem to have enough calories left over to build up a bulk. That doesn't take away from the fact that the work is punishingly hard. Chris knows this all too well. 'The routine of crabbing is a tough job. I'm forty-one doing the work that people of half my age do. I have a daughter who's three years old and I get home and she wants to play or read a book but I'm too tired. We don't have much of a social life because I'm too tired. It ages people. Most of the people around here look older than they are because they work so hard. Maybe I make about four hundred dollars a week after taxes which isn't too bad but the season only lasts six months of the year so that's what makes it so difficult.'

Leaving Carl and Chris to eat their lunch I went to meet an older breed of waterman altogether. Walking to Elmer Evans's house I noticed just how many birds there were; everywhere you looked there they were! Herons of a near definitive range of species decorated mailboxes, ducks appeared on walls, egrets stood sentinel in the gardens, optimistic goose decoys sat on lawns to tempt their living brethren in to graze, wooden woodpeckers clung to fenceposts, not to mention the real birds. A spray of small birds lifted off a bird feeder in one garden, including a beautifully plumaged slate-coloured junco, a member of the sunbird family – a purple finch which looked like a dowdy and dull brown bird that had been freshly dipped in raspberry juice.

Elmer Evans is eighty-one and a great yarner, a teller of tales. Known to many as Captain, he learned to work the water in the company of his uncle Noah (pronounced Noyee) who made him a twelve-foot skiff. He showed me a model he had made. In his younger days he enjoyed the company of Edward Jones, a next-door neighbour. 'We would paddle around together – go out every day. Old Edward Jones would come out every day on to to the crab wharf and say "hard off boys you're going to be drowned, you're going to be drowned," and we'd go out every day and capsize both of us – we could swim like fish.'

His father was drowned, frozen out on the ice in 1926 on the Potomac, leaving his mother with six children to feed and clothe.

Elmer's got an sixteen-foot skiff with an eight-horsepower Yamaha engine and a little winding rig with a five-horsepower hydraulic system for the winding gear.

'I trotline. Yesterday I had twenty-three dollars' worth and today I had seventy-two but I had fresh chicken necks on today and yesterday they were old. Chicken legs are the best but it don't last long. Bait don't last long – a third of yesterday's bait had gone by today. Bull lips are good from the slaughterhouse – they're tough, they'll stay on there a while.'

Elmer uses two lines – each one being 2,000 foot long – with loops holding the bait spaced about six feet apart. 'Most of the time the crabs are different to what the scrapers and potters are catching. Most of the time the trotlined crabs are harder and most times they run bigger, big clubby-claws, ones with big biters on them – they're all rust coloured, the bottoms of the aprons and all. Some I call them "marble belly" – their bellies are white and shiny.

'There have been some mighty hard years. I done all right until I was forty-five and then the arthritis got so bad and almost knocked me out altogether. I spent a long time in hospital in Baltimore. I had two spinal operations in '81 – one of the discs in my back had exploded and fragmented. There were two seven-hour operations and I had half my stomach out in '59.

'After that I fell two or three times and one time on the bow of my skiff right backward; it's a wonder I didn't break my back. On October thirteenth, 1984, the Full Gospel Fellowship came over and healed at the store. A man laid his hands on me and after he prayed and asked me how I felt. Well, I bent over and touched the floor with my fingertips and I hadn't done that in thirty-five years. Even though I hobbled there with a cane I came back with the cane under my arm!

'I've come down that Bay more than once – it be so rough it wear you right out. I'd say, "Lord surely you can make smoother than this, I'm getting tired. Lord my arms are wearing out – just let me have a little bit of relief," and it wouldn't be five minutes 'fore you come there in a place where it was almost smooth. I come from Annapolis one time – was steering with one hand – I'd lost all the use of my other arm, every bit of it, and it was a rough time – one of the longest trips on that Bay. The Lord travels with me. I put on the full armour of God before I go out.'

He laughed when I suggested that most people put their feet up at his age. 'I was born in 1918 but I don't feel old.'

Elmer has seen a bit of the world way beyond Tangier Sound. He served in the Navy aboard U.S.S. Chaffey, a destroyer. A Japanese Moro sword hangs on the wall as testimony to this chapter in his life. Not only did he survive the war but he also survived a considerable dose of strychnine given him by a local doctor to cure boils and carbuncles! He has also seen the century ring some changes on Smith Island. He remembers when Smith streets were dark before the coming of electric light, when everybody had white picket fences.

What does he think about when he's out by himself? 'Thinking about different verses in the Bible, talking to the Lord lots of the time. I look over that eastern edge before that

46

sun comes out and them great big clouds there, I say Lord, could this be the day that you're coming? 'Cause he's coming. Lots of people don't believe him, but when he comes, and if they don't believe then they're gone, they're lost.'

Many of his recollections are about his youth because Elmer is well into his second childhood. As I prepared to leave, he turned back the clock a good few years.

'I lived with my uncle Everett once in the middle of a big freeze and there were big flocks of duck; it was 1936. Me and his oldest boy, from beginning of October to middle of March, we'd go gunning all the time and I never remember going up the stairs that you didn't have wildfowl hanging there – baldpates, blue bills, sprigtails, old squaws, dippers.'

Old squaws are also known as 'southerlies' echoing their call which can sound like 'suth, suth, sutherly' having flown south from nesting grounds on Baffin island and Greenland, where their down is avidly gathered by the Innuit, their feathers rivalling eiderdown for warmth. Favouring water far from shore, these ducks congregate in rafts, their white plumage brighter than snow.

That evening I was sitting in Rukes, eating a tasty crab sandwich. A waterman, catching sight of my notebook, asked 'Are you working hard?' I thought of the backbreaking labours of Carl, Chris and Elmer and shook my head.

Chapter 5

WOMEN TOGETHER

'Love, men, is not bringing your wife an extra bushel to pick.'

Smith Islander

In a quiet corner of what little real land there is on Tylerton stands a small white building which houses the mini crab processing plant. Here, fifteen deft and diligent pickers produce some 5,000 pounds of crabmeat annually. This year's president of the co-op, Betty, talks me through the process which might as well be eye-microsurgery for all I genuinely understand of the deftly moving hands and slowly dismantling crab. She makes it look simple. 'We opened in 1996, due to Health Department regulations. My job is to make sure that the building gets cleaned properly and that there are the right supplies in stock. They wanted us to build a parking lot and we didn't understand why because we don't have any cars here – all we have are bicycles and gold carts! Our husbands catches our crabs and we shuck them. There are fifteen women picking. Probably averaging about two pounds of crabmeat a session, some do three or four, working from two bushels each. Mine is usually about two. There's no great skill to it. All you have to do is learn how to cut 'em. You just take the back off, you cut the mouth away and the devils – the lungs – and then you cut the fins off, cut the crab in half and you pull the meat out of the sections. Then you take the other half and pick the meat out of it.'

There are different sections to a crab. Each meat is different and has particular uses. The meat from the claw is the brownest and is the best for dips and soups and also happens to be the most inexpensive to buy. 'Lump' describes the largest pieces of meat from the body, found adjacent to the backfin and this is top-of-the-range stuff, the most expensive form of crabmeat – not quite caviar but equally delicious. 'Backfin' is the white body meat including the lump and large flakes. This is used for crab cakes and crab imperial while 'special' is the word used to refer to flakes of white body meat other than 'lump' which are good for crab cakes, soups, casseroles and dips.

The plant rings with peals of womens' laughter. The women work close enough to one another for a hushed-voiced conversation to be unintelligible to the rest – not that the place lends itself to secrets. This is the island's CNN newsroom, everyone an anchorwoman, each able to shuck a crab and run through the day's headlines simultaneously.

'We certainly don't talk about crabs all day,' Betty emphasises. 'We talk about everything – it's been mainly Bill Clinton here today.'

Clinton had been unashamedly lying on a dozen networks that morning and one got the feeling that here was a man who would do anything to divert attention from his difficulties, even bomb a far-off country. Some smokescreen. There were already some good jokes circulating the island. I liked the one about Bill Clinton being challenged about the famous cigar – that it had been a Cuban one, despite the U.S.-imposed embargo on imports from Castro's Cuba. Clinton admitted it was but added '. . . look at it another way – I'm just burning their crops.' The women had views, counterviews, small-town America's reponse to scandal along the corridors of power.

'Before the co-op we worked in our outhouses,' continued Mrs President – 'what you call sheds on the mainland – where you keep your lawnmowers and all that. Well, we'd section it off and that's where we picked our crabs.

'Every evening we have a lady comes in and we have devotions – reads a part out of the Bible, and sometimes we sing hymns. I think it's brought us all closer together, we all harmonise together.

'A lot of women come at different hours: some start at three in the morning, some come in the evening and we pick from three to three-thirty in the morning until eight or nine o clock at night.'

Betty took me through some of the destinations whither the crabs were bound. 'The crabs go all over – to Dewey Beach, Delaware gets a lot of it, Linton Seafood in Crisfield gets some, we have a lot of personal orders that we fill. Dwight Marshall who lives here has a lot of buyers in Ocean City.'

I was then introduced to Louise Clayton who was sitting one bench along.

'I've lived here almost twenty-eight years. I've got two sons – they both got married last year and both live on the mainland. Most of the younger ones move away – they don't stay on the island any more. The water business is getting very slow and there's many more advantages on the mainland. When they leave you don't have much of a population left. But I'm not pessimistic. We keep on going with our way of life that we've always known over here.

'I met my husband through his cousin because they went to school together up in Baltimore. I was around twenty-one when I moved to Smith, and it wasn't that great an adjustment. Sometimes when your mother would call to say she'd gone to the store to hit on a bargain you'd feel a bit cut off. When you go over to the mainland you have to get a month's supply of things.'

Louise confirmed that the plant also doubles as Gossip Central. 'You don't even need to look at the crabs as you talk to someone. That means you can do a lot of talking . . .'

The Claytons are a very small family in Tylerton. 'It's just my husband and I and his sister because both his parents are deceased. The church fills the vacuum left by family. Your church is your main thing – it's more like your town council, mayor or whatever: the church is the centre.'

Her neighbour on the bench, Joan Corbin, was listening to a Walkman when I moved over to talk to her. For her also, the church is a fulcrum: 'I like our church and the church family. If I would have any problems – financial problems or anything else – I could go to our church and they would be there for us –

50

to help us out. I know everybody on here and they know me – sometimes that can be bad – but it can be good too. We rely on each other for strength and support – if we ever need help the community is always there for us.'

Joan thinks that life is much improved by the co-op.

'It's made picking crabs easier. Husbands don't have to worry about steaming the crabs; it's made fun to pick with the other women. There's just me and my husband. I've lived here all my life – we've been married seven years and we don't have any children.

'I can't imagine living anywhere else but here. It can be hard, like doing shopping, but we don't have to worry about crime and drive-by shootings. I worry about my husband though – it's worrisome in the wintertime when the water freezes over and it's blowing hard – it's worrisome then – but in the summer it's not too bad because they don't spend so much time out on the water – they're usually in about noon but in the winter they're out all day until evening.

'We work so hard in the summer that we need the winter to take it easy. We usually use the winter to do our house-cleaning and catch up on things that we let go all summer long because we work so hard.

'Boy we work! I used to get up earlier, at three or four, but now I'm on dialysis and get up about six o' clock to go to work. I put in about nine or ten hours a day, five days a week, not picking on Saturday unless we really have a lot of crabs.

'It's pretty good money in crabpicking. They charge seventeen or eighteen dollars in the shop. I get thirteen but I actually get eleven because I have to give two dollars on the pound back to the co-op. Now as far as my husband goes, I think the dealers could give more money for their crabs. It seems like when there's not many crabs they get a better price and then when a lot of crabs come then they cut the price so much that they hardly make anything.'

In front of her is a white polystyrene tub which contains sixteen ounces of prime picked crab meat. 'If the crabs are good crabs it usually takes me about twenty to twenty-five

51

minutes to pick a pound. I learned to do it when I was twelve or thirteen so I was pretty young. Every woman in here – if you will notice them – they do a little something different. I don't think no two in here picks crabs alike – so everybody has their own different style. Some of 'em says if you do this you can do it quicker but I'm so used to my own technique if I try something different it ends up taking me longer.

'We usually have supper early – about three thirty. We go to bed around nine o'clock, sometimes a little earlier than that. I guess if some other kind of career choice would come to the island I would probably choose that, but I wouldn't leave the island. Sometimes we take for granted being here all the time – sometimes we get a lot of visitors and sightseers who tell us how beautiful it is and it causes us to stop and really look at how beautiful it is here, but we take it for granted most of the time because we're so used to it.'

The women were all smiling as I left, each woman working still, their fingers weaving invisible patterns over the small graveyards of broken carapace.

Chapter 6

THE ISLE OF WESLEY'S HEIRS

Gwae inni wybod y geiriau heb adnabod y Gair/A gwerthu ein henaid am doffi a chonffeti ffair

(Woe that we should know the words without recognising the Word/And sell our soul for toffee-apples and fairground baubles)

D. Gwenallt Jones, 'Ar Gyfeiliorn'

The first Methodist missionaries such as Francis Asbury who came to America were good and efficient messengers, and the word spread like brushfire in places. It certainly managed to light the flame of faith on Smith where Methodism is still one of the defining features of the community.

The local lynchpin of Methodism and of its revivals was Joshua Thomas, the so-called Parson of the Islands. Born in Potato Neck in Somerset County, he was the son of a schoolteacher-turned-sailor. His father died of a dog bite, leaving Joshua in the care of a dypsomaniacal stepfather whose love of drink – brought on by his house being burned down by refugees from the war – was only rivalled by his disregard for his family. The stepfather ultimately drowned and when Joshua came of age he went to work for a waterman, a Smith islander with a very definite moral backbone, who was the wellspring of Joshua's faith: 'As far as he knew in what religion consisted, he practised it, and taught it to me. I learned a great many good things from him.' The young man who had displayed a definite talent for dancing now showed a true understanding of the ways of the water. But his real forte was to be revealed when the normally shy boy spoke publicly at one of the testimony meetings. From thenceforward he visited the islands of the Chesapeake in his great log canoe, *The Methodist*, described as the largest canoe afloat. It measured between twenty feet and thirty feet in length and was five foot wide. It had been manufactured from a tree so vast in size that when it was felled the sound was 'like the roar and reverberation of heavy ordnance, and shook the ground for many miles around.'

The island's remembrancer Jennings Evans imagines his ancestors making their decisions: 'They said, "That's the kind of religion we need. We don't have to have a priest: we can talk right to God." So this kind of religion, where you kneel down and pray straight to the Man, they thought that was great, and it was ideal for somebody living on these outer reaches. It was just practical and it caught fire.'

Adam Wallace, in his biography of Joshua Thomas, *The Parson of the Islands* (1961), describes the announcement of the preacher's arrival:

> *The arrival of the preachers, and the hour for public worship, is made known on Smith's, as on nearby Tangier island, by hoisting a flag at the little church. The signal flag was procured by the Sons of Temperance, who have a flourishing division there. It bears their motto – 'Union Bound' – and where unfurled to the breeze may be seen from every part of the island.*

According to Wallace, Joshua possessed a 'natural roughness, a polished diamond of the first order, to whom lawyers, judges, doctors and preachers gave more heed than they would to the most cultured man in the community.' He was a simple man, who did not have a stentorian voice like so many other bearers of the faith – although some accounts hold that when 'aroused to exhortation' his voice could be heard a mile distant. Yet he communicated something urgent and sometimes 'shouted himself happy.' Wound up into a frenzy, he would engender a sort of mass hysteria and 'under pressure of the general shout, the sleepers gave way and the crowd fell through the floor.' This put me in mind of Daniel Rowland, Thomas's equivalent in Wales, who could work a crowd into such frenzied faith that they would start jumping. Indeed his followers, who would number as many as 6,000 of a Sunday, and would come from all four corners of the country, came to be known as 'jumpers.' One day they worked themselves up into such a pitch that the balcony on which they were standing collapsed. Methodist chapels need reinforced building materials.

Some of the stories about Joshua Thomas beggar belief: how, for example, he could walk across the Sound in white socks and not get them soiled; or there is the story about an old man who was told he needed to eat fish to get well. It was a winter when the Bay was locked by ice, yet Joshua punched a hole in the ice-sheet and pulled out a striped bass for the sick man's supper.

Perhaps this charismatic man's most famous moment came after the British fleet made Tangier Sound the centre of their operations in the Chesapeake. Thomas struck up a relationship with the British Admiral and successfully defended the trees around the Tabernacle grounds from naval axes. Then in the summer of 1814, as the British made their preparations to attack Baltimore, Thomas was invited to exhort the men. He addressed 12,000 of them, telling them in no uncertain terms that God had told him that they could not take the city. And fail they did, in an attack which was to be immortalised in Francis Scott Key's poem, which would of course evolve into the National Anthem.

Later in his life Joshua Thomas took a bad fall which resulted in his being confined to a wheelchair. He died at the age of seventy-five. His epitaph reads:

> Come all my friends, as you pass by,
> Behold the place where I do lie;
> As you are now, so once was I;
> Remember you are born to die.

Methodism changed the way of life on Smith – it found favour as the religion of ordinary people because of its belief in an active God who affects nature, its encouragement of self-discipline and hard work, its message of forgiveness and hope and its focus on community. A cursory glance at the church classifications in the Yellow Pages for Somerset and Worcester Counties in Maryland shows the lasting and varied presence of Methodism, covering as they do a huge range of denominations – with Methodist, United Methodist and African Methodist Episcopal taking their place among the Southern Baptists, the Lutherans and Mennonites, the Unitarian Universalists, the Pentecostal and Nazarene churches.

John Wesley sent missionaries such as Francis Asbury to a pretty godless place when he dispatched them to the Delmarva just before the War of Independence. Ignorance reigned supreme hereabouts. One missionary, intent on sharing his zeal with the inhabitants of Somerset county – the mainland for Smith – asked a man 'Do you know Jesus Christ?', to which the man replied that he knew neither the man nor where he lived.

But the Methodist message of hard work, temperance, share and share alike, and the importance of both family and community, found willing ears and ready converts. The number of Methodists on Delmarva went from zero to 10,000 within a couple of decades of the Revolutionary War. In 1784, estimates had it that a third of all American Methodists lived on the peninsula. Not for nothing was it called Methodism's 'garden.' It took root, and grew, blossomed like topsy.

In 1808, the first Methodist meeting on Smith was held at Fog Point, home of 'King' Richard Evans, with Joshua Thomas in attendance. The following year 'bush' meetings – so called because they were held under the trees and stars – were held by Evans and his brother Solomon:

> And kneeling down, the evangelist broke into passionate pleadings, which seemed to reach the very hearts of his hearers. The upturned faces flushed and worked with some strong yearning; and as if with one impulse the whole congregation burst into a volume of song, drowning the prayers of the evangelist, who rose from his knees and joined his voice to the impassioned harmony . . .

At last it ceased, and a breathless silence fell upon the
meeting – the very air seemed full of a throbbing expectation;
until from some mysterious depths there floated in upon their
consciousness a power, an influence, *indescribable, but*
strongly felt as if an invisible presence were amongst them.
The Spirit! for whose advent they had prayed so long. The
Spirit! who had raised so many of their friends from sin to
righteousness, from darkness to light had come . . .

This, however, is not a description of a revival meeting in
America but rather of a fictional meeting in Wales, where
Methodist ministers, like their brothers on the other side of
the Atlantic, set whole communities ablaze with religious
fervour. That imagined meeting comes from *The Queen of the*
Rushes, a novel by a once bestselling but now largely forgotten
Welsh novelist called Allen Raine, the pseudonym of the
wonderfully named Anne Adaliza Puddicombe and gives a
vivid account of the emotion and ecstasy of such a meeting.

Here's an account of one such American meeting:

The sudden and spontaneous outburst that then rolled out
over the waters and rang through the woods . . . was
indescribable. As by an earthquake shock, sinners fell
prostrate; . . . the sensation of that shout was experienced on
board the vessels in the crowded harbour. Some, unconscious
of all surrounding things, mingled with the amazed throng
and joined the general rejoicing, having paddles on their
shoulders, which, after leaping on the shore, they forgot to
leave with the canoes.

Since 1887 a grove of trees at Ewell, the Wilson Butler
Tabernacle and camp ground, has been used for the camp
meeting. In their heyday, camp meetings exerted such a pull
that the faithful attendants filled thirty frame tents or cottages
and a boarding house for up to sixty guests. Even nowadays the
womenfolk of Smith get up at five in the morning to cook
chickens and turkeys for those attending the camp meeting,
although the tradition is slowly dying out because there are
now three restaurants on the island.

I met the current pastor of the island, the Reverend Ashley Maxwell, a black Barbadian who is sixty years of age, in the parsonage built to replace the one burned down in 1937.

'I came in 1989 when they were looking for a camp meeting speaker. Camp meetings are both a homecoming and a declaration of faith. They occur between the last Sunday of July and the last Sunday of August. There'll be a gospel concert and it all has a crusade type appeal. It's a chance to re-examine their spiritual lives.

'The people of Smith had seen me in action then, and I came over every year after 1989 for about a week to preach something. In 1995 they petitioned the bishop asking for me to come to Smith now that their own pastor had resigned, and the bishop pointed out that in the Methodist church you don't get to choose your own pastor but he'd consider it because it's so hard to get a white church to take a cross-racial appointment. I only know of four or five cross-racial ministeries and most of them come from the West Indies. My ministry's now almost over. I came here to get away from the mad rush and the race for appointments.

'The people over here are strongly evangelical Methodists. You know, the Methodist belief system allows for all kinds of pluralism which allows for anything from liberals to charismatics. I'm one of those what you might call a liberal evangelical – I don't believe in a literal scripture at very point and turn. I believe you need hermeneutics, the history, the languages, you need the findings of archaeology and history to be able to decipher certain scriptures properly, but in addition to that I'm also a very strong evangelical and these people are very strong evangelical people – they believe in emphasising a social gospel; they believe in the salvation message – people ought to repent – turn around and get right with God – that sort of thing. I don't preach much about heaven and hell; and ask me why and I'll say it's because I don't know much about either. All I know is that from what little Jesus said, I would like to make my choice on those words, but that's what they liked about my style. I wasn't one of these Methodist preachers who wanted to talk a lot of about philosophy and politics and social issues. These people want you to go to the Bible and make it speak to them where they live today – to make it speak to the ills and the problems of the world and seek possible solutions, and I think that's what got 'em.'

At Tylerton they have a few who have allegedly spoken in tongues. Reverend Maxwell doesn't hold with it: 'The scriptures say that if you can't interpret what they're saying they would have to keep quiet.

'I use the lectionary – we all do in the Methodist church – so all the scriptures read in America tomorrow will be the same as those read all around the world. I do an exegesis on the scriptures of the day. Seldom will I digress from the lectionary.

'Self-discipline is pretty central. The Law Book of the Methodist church is called the Book of Discipline. The discipline of the Methodists today is nothing to when John Welsey was alive. The message of Methodism in terms of self-discipline harmonised with the requirements for success in this environment. If these same people had settled in the mountains they would be different. Here the wind, tide, the seafood – everything about the environment – has come together to dictate which direction their discipline will take – the discipline and the environment went hand in hand. And don't forget there hasn't been another religion on this island – on a Sunday morning there may be Catholics, Lutheran, Pentecostals, Adventists – one here, one there, of different denominations but this is still a Methodist place. Methodism on Smith Island is more ecumenical, but it's still eighty per cent Methodist.

'Since World War II people have been leaving here – before that there were between eight and nine hundred people here but many went to Baltimore to work on ships and munitions and so on. Even when I came here in '89 there were still about five hundred people but many have died and others have had to leave to look for employment. Many from Smith Island have been drifting to Florida, to New Jersey and Pennsylvania but they come back for their children to be christened or to be baptised or for themselves to be buried.

'Here we have an open-air religion, a Christianity which is more aware of the environment. In a big city rain falls, snow falls, sun sets, sun rises, everything passes in its season and people hardly ever pay attention to them all. Over here, because of where they live, the people are more conscious of the environment than the average person in the city because it determines their daily living, and it also brings to their consciousness that there must be some mastermind in this universe on whom they are extremely dependent. They might say 'Let's go fishing.' That will be followed by 'Let's wait till tomorrow and see if the good Lord gives us the weather.'

On Smith Island, society is focused on the family, which is both fulcrum and bedrock. 'The importance of family, well I think a lot of it has to do with their history. They came to this New World back in the 1600s. Maryland was ceded to the Catholics – to Lord Baltimore and that bunch – and some of those who came out as Protestants said, "By George we will not be ruled by Catholics." Now that didn't cause any war that I know of, but a lot of the people that came up to Smith came to protect their Protestant belief system – they didn't want anything to do with Catholicism. Of course, Maryland became more Protestant than Catholic, but the people in those days were a lot more intolerant than they are today. So you have an attitude of people who came out to an island in the middle of the Chesapeake Bay twelve or thirteen miles from each shore as a living, enduring act of defiance against being ruled by anybody else. By so doing, we're probably still the only island with any sizeable population without a bridge – by so doing they cut themselves off from the mainland for many years.

'By being cut off from the mainland there was a lot of intermarrying – biologically and socially – generation after generation, which has maintained the same concept of freedom. That concept of freedom has joined itself together with certain biological predispositions so that . . . and I don't want to say this in a bad way – they are all alike. They don't just feel a bond because there's some sort of economic or socially satisfying reason – so even if they're from Tangier

Island or somewhere else, they really eventually develop a blood bondedness so that they're disposed towards a particular lifestyle.

'To hook up with that, they will tell you there has never been a murder on the island by another islander – the police have shot a few and so on – and I know from experience that if there's vandalism they don't like to report the ones they think did it. They'll complain to one another but they don't want the law out there interfering with the people of Smith Island. One reason why there's not been a lot of crimes committed on Smith Island is if you commit a crime the chances of getting away with it are near impossible – where are you going to go? – so I think a lot of these small factors put together form a perspective that has now presented itself as a strong family bond. It became necessary because of environmental and geographical restrictions, so that they became like one big family.'

In many respects the Reverend's native Caribbean island of Barbados and his adoptive Smith are very similar. Barbados – where the Reverend Maxwell was baptised by the Moravians – is 'much bigger and it's not marshy but the history and the customs are British. These people here started as British – they are now American, but that British flavour has remained with them. My home and here share water and boats, fishermen and a people that are very isolated in a sense. If you go anywhere in the world you'll recognise a Barbadian by his accent.' The Smith accent would be hard to mistake either.

Whilst Barbados has a full structure of government, with a Senate and an Elected House of Assembly dating back to 1627, Smith has no real political structure for organising its affairs locally. This vacuum is filled by the church.

'The church is the nearest thing to a government that the island has. I recently started a community council but they have not taken to that very well because they still expect the church to be the decision maker, the trendsetter, to take the initiative on internal affairs and the preacher, of course, is the unofficial mayor – I don't like that too much. We are part of a

61

county, we are part of a state, we have county laws, we have state laws but we don't have local laws.

'The church collects money to run certain aspects of the island's life. They go house to house, door to door, so there are seasonal peaks reflecting their takings on the water. Street lights on Smith – the church pays for them. Drilling the new well was administered and paid for from church coffers.'

'And here some mainland laws simply don't apply, or, rather, are not applied.' They say they you can recognise the Reverend's car by the fact that it is the only one with tax plates. On an unpoliced island there is no one to check.

'The people out here, because of a long tradition of rebelliousness, resent laws that come from higher up. They want to be a law unto themselves and I do preach that from the pulpit from time to time . . . that they can't have too much lawlessness. When they go to school on the mainland people pick on them, which is one reason why you don't have racism here.'

The Reverend's life isn't entirely island-bound. He has a large garden near the town of Berlin on the mainland and spends two days a week 'out there in the sun with the mosquitoes, digging and growing a lot of vegetables, tilling, and my wife spends a lot of time babysitting the grandchildren.'

As befits a fisher of men, the Reverend Maxwell is also a keen fisherman. 'I catch flounder and hardheads or crokers and sea trout. The big sport fish around here is rockfish, striped bass. If you catch a big one it's a lot of fun if it doesn't get away. I fish the Bay where the salt water and fresh water are mingling for fifty miles.'

The congregations at his three island churches remain fairly strong. The big Christian festivals such as Easter, Christmas and Mother's Day draw big crowds with, on average, somewhere in the order of seventy-five to ninety attendees. Last Easter there were 150 at the nine o'clock service. He holds two services usually, a sunrise service at six o'clock and one at nine o'clock in the morning. Ordinary Sunday attendances at the 'capital', Ewell, 'can number as many as seventy or eighty but usually hover around the forty-five and fifty mark. Here in Ewell there are forty houses that are empty.'

Rhodes Point might peak at fifty on Easter Sunday with an average of between thirty-two and thirty-five.

'Christmas is a big thing here. Sometimes it gets pretty close to being non-Christian. A lot of these symbols are pagan. Commercialism preaches everything here, yessir.

'When I arrived in 1989 the mainland had already arrived. You will find these people jumping on a boat and going to the mainland to protest "no liquor store". On the other hand, anytime you come over on the boat you see the liquor loaded up on the boat. When I first came over here there was liquor, there was drugs, all kinds of sexual immorality – it's all here, the mainland is here.

'It's not apparent and it's a minority viewpoint, but every evil you can think of on the mainland is here – but in very small doses. We're talking about abuses such as alcoholism. Some of the young men on this island who have to be referred out for treatment are awfully sick in terms of their addiction to alcohol. I call that an evil when you're so addicted to alcohol or drugs. One of our twelve year olds, he's diabetic. The ambulance was called in for him but when they got to hospital they found he had tried marijuana and vodka. Of course I'm purposely not saying some things – I can say it in a general sense – incest for instance – you find it in all three parts – it's not well known because there's not too many but I call incest evil – the evil of child abuse.

'Like so many super-religious communities there is a surface appearance and there is an under-the-surface appearance where it is not usually as high and holy – that's why Bibles are so necessary – because a lot of wrongdoing is here.

'We formed a prayer group in 1987, which was the hundredth camp meeting, and we formed a group of just men who go to church on a Saturday night and pray. When we started out the most we had was nine but now we're down to four.

'A friend of mine fish-trapped for years. I was talking to him, I said, "Catching any herring over there this year J.D.?" He said, "They're not doing neither thing in the world – the scarcest herring has been for years and years." That winter we prayed that the Lord would send herring for the fishermen and that next spring they had the greatest run of herring they've had in the last twenty-five years.'

Yet no abundance of fish can compare with the underwater legions described by Captain John Smith who said that 'in diverses places that abundance of fish, lying so thick with their heads above the water, as for want of nets (our barge driving amongst them) we attempted to catch them with a frying pan: but we found it a bad instrument to catch fish with.'

I left the Reverend Maxwell to write his sermon.

Let's hope the sermon he penned that afternoon elicited the same delicious reaction as that of Uncle Haney . . .

Uncle Haney, a famous patriarch of the island, had a way with words. He'd coin them at a fair old rate and his speech was entirely his own. This is how he complimented a visiting preacher on his sermon:

'I tell you, brother, you had a mighty bunctious tex' tonight. Why, sir, if you'd combusticated at that dyin' rate a little longer, I'd a splodified right out the co-sanctum! In that way and form, sir, you got things in a solid smother. Why hain't they made you a Bishop long ago?'

There is no evidence that Uncle Haney ever did 'splodify'. At least one hopes not.

Chapter 7

TIME WITH THE WAVE

There is a fish that swims in the sea;
It has two arms to make it free;
It carries twelve men every day
And has two eyes to see its way.

Riddle by Mrs B.F. Marsh, Smith Island

I met Waverley Evans, known by many as Wave, at cockcrow in his shanty near the main dock in Tylerton. The blustery wind kept us inside and off the water for a while, which gave us time to chew the fat. He is a sprightly seventy-two year old who has spent most of his long life on the water. If the age of our parents is any sign of longevity, then Waverley has at least a score of years left to him, because his mother is very much alive, at the redoubtable age of ninety-two, and lives with his younger brother in Dover, Delaware. Waverley has skin the colour of a beech nut and a sharp, somewhat aquiline nose that gives him the outline of a terrapin. The alert look in his eyes belies his age. On one of his leathery, almost silurian arms, there is a tattoo of a flag with a heart set in it, etched there when he was in the Army, when he was 'young and carefree'. It would seem from this quiet man's disposition that his old heart beats out a young man's lust for life.

He was with the Army during the war, and travelled to Minnesota and also to Texas where he felt very far from home, not least because he was far from water.

According to his fellow islanders, Waverley is so quiet that he might as well have taken vows of silence. The man I met was talkative, garrulous even, a man who's been hoarding stories and experiences much as a squirrel hides away its autumn store. He first tells me about his family, pursing his wrinkled lips and letting slip a thin note of regret in his voice.

'My oldest daughter Sandy has a beauty parlour in Crisfield – she has it right in her home. She has one child – I have one granddaughter – her husband is from Ewell and they moved to Crisfield. He's a postmaster. My second is Connie and lives at Rhodes Point – she does a lot of work cleaning, painting and delivers the mail and works in Alan Tyler's restaurant as a cook. They have one son Kim, and he's a carpenter in Salisbury and he's doing pretty good. My third is Jane – she lives in Ewell and is the schoolteacher after going to college in Salisbury State. Missie Margaret; she's the telephone lady – the manager of the telephone building in Ewell. That's my family.'

It is also a familiar family diaspora. Fewer children stay with their families on the island anymore. The writer John Berger said that the great migration of the twentieth century has been that from the village to the city. That phenomenon has been seen on Smith as it has in São Páolo. The phone book for Crisfield and other places on the Delmarva Peninsula is alive with Evanses and Tylers and Marshalls, the island names transplanted to the safety of land and the proximity of drive-thru convenience.

His father took him to work the water at a very early age. 'I've been crabbing since I was big enough to walk. My father used to take us, me and my twin brother Weldon, out crabbing with him and we would have a little bunk – we called it a booby house – up in the bow of the boat and we would fool around, you know? Sometimes we would make little boats out of bottles and stuff like that, and we would play around on the boat until it got light and the tide got down. We had a little skiff and he would put us out in it and we would go in and out crabbing until it was time to come home and he would come and get us, take our crabs on the boat and bring us on in. We had a great time. We used to look forward to it. He was a man that'd let us do things, you know what I mean? He didn't tell us "You do this, you do that" – he let us do it on our own. Lot of times we'd get in a jam, but most of the time we would come out on top.

'I remember one morning when we were going down on the end of the wharf and it was slippery – it had rained that night. I fell overboard and I were hanging onto a pole and he says "swim, there's your boats right there," so I had to let go the pole and I just swum to the boat. "See," he said, "nothing to be afraid of!"'

Not only was his father liberal in his ways but he also had more than a hint of St. Francis of Assissi about him. On an island where empathy with nature is a given, Waverley's father had something else – a genuinely gifted way with animals.

'My father ran a crab house right directly across from the dock and these little birds – we'd call them shanty birds – little swallows used to build their nest in there, and he got 'em so tame that they would come to pitch on his knee or on the arm of his chair and he would talk to them. Their little heads would go back and forth as if they were listening to him – he was a gentle person. I miss him a lot – he didn't have much of an education but he was wise in many ways; he was a great father and he taught me so many things.'

Waverley is the inheritor of his father's connectedness with the wild. Standing on the boardwalk outside his shanty he whistled gently, the piping sound carrying across the stillness of the early morning marshes. Suddenly a bird rose, Phoenix-like, from the grey reeds, flapped steadily right towards us and landed on a piling. It was a black-crowned night heron, known locally as a sedge hen or bumcutter, and I had never seen one before. It took a septuagenarian crab fisherman with magic in his whistle to show me one. This was birdspotting made very easy. Waverley had christened his young avian charge 'Scout'.

The bird in front of us was a young bird and therefore did not sport the adult's sooty black cap with its summer accessory of elegant white plumes. Scout had a vaguely punk-rockerlike appearance, his head still graced with tufts of juvenile feathers, which stood up a little, as if startled by electric shock. Black-crowned night herons usually feed at dusk, but this one seemed perfectly at ease with being abroad so early in the day. Short-legged and stocky, with a thick

67

daggerlike bill, Scout's plumage was dull brown streaked with white and buff – the perfect camouflage for a bird which skulks in the reeds and cordgrass.

'He started coming here about a month or so ago. I saw him on the pole and I shouted come on in here and get something to eat,' Waverley tells me.

I refrained from pointing out that if talking to oneself is the first sign of madness then conversing with herons must surely count as conclusive evidence. 'Finally', Waverley continued, 'I cut a piece of crab in two and dangled it and he'd look and finally he got up enough nerve, I guess you call it, to come in close and so I threw it to him and he come to pick it up so now he looks for me every morning. Many times in the afternoon and the evening when there's time to fish the soft crabs out and go home, he'll show up then and see if he can get something to eat. He's sort of got used to it now, I guess. In the morning he waits for the light to come. He gets up early.' He certainly does. I look at my watch. It is still unconscionably early.

Soon the purple and petrol-blue snakes of cigarette smoke coiled and settled around us to form a fug in the little shed. Waverley gets through a pack a day. Some solace might be sought in the line of Welsh poet, Peter Finch: 'If God hadn't meant us to smoke he wouldn't have given us lungs', but on such a staunchly devout and Methodist island I think that such a sentiment would be a seed cast on stony ground. Waverley sincerely believes the cigarettes stunted his growth.

We talked about retirement. At home my farmer friends, from Llanddeusant to Llanrwst, are almost congenitally unable to give up work, and their counterparts in Chesapeake Bay, the crab fishermen, seem to suffer from the same addiction to the Protestant work ethic. 'I guess an old waterman never really retires until he's stretched out six foot. We try to keep busy. Of course, in the wintertime we used to oyster and have to live on the boat round Annapolis and different places, but the last three years I just stay home and piddle around and do odd jobs – I'm sort of the fix-it man.' Waverley's 'piddling around' is another man's hard work.

He also makes lots of things and you might well look at Waverley's pieces as little works of art – simple, primitive and affecting. He makes little ladies out of crab floats which can make you laugh. He gives them white aprons and little nets – and they smile as if they're coming to the end of the last bushel of the day. Sometimes Waverley works with materials Providence itself has given him. One day he found some sharks' teeth caught in his oyster tongs. Another day he caught the complete skull of a fish, and a friend on Solomon's Island suggested taking it to the museum, where 'they done a lot of research on it and they sent me a paper.' Waverley had found a prehistoric shark's head 'dated about twelve million years old. That's one of his teeth, I suppose – teeth about twelve million years old!'

One of Waverley's other skills involves making clocks, which he decorates with the Native American arrowheads he finds on the shore. They hang as serried ranks on the wall behind him, each telling a different time, as befits an island where time itself seems a little unhurried. He can turn his hand to anything, it seems. He has made pencil holders out of an old piece of two-by-four – 'This is a piece of wood out of one of the pews, maybe a hundred years old or more.' He has also made lots of small nets: '. . . We use them for dipping out soft crabs – that's how we used to catch crabs – standing on the bow of the boat and just scooping them up in the net. Used to be a real old way of life but the grasses are disappearing and the water stays thick all the time. I think the grass used to filter the mud, but now the water stays so thick you can hardly see the bottom most of the time.'

Dip nets were once the principal tool for catching soft shells and peeler crabs in the Chesapeake. The watermen would pole along the shore in a skiff and, if necessary, wade in the water to catch a mess. Others used dip nets when mudlarking in shallow guts and coves.

Waverley knows that this technique – which calls for a combination of adept handling of the boat, a trapeze artist's sense of balance and an unfailing eye for a crab's swimming

69

strokes – is rapidly disappearing. 'Pots and scrapes are the main crabbing now,' he tells me with a certain wistfulness.

'I fish seventy-five crab pots and that's all I do right now. I sure have seen a lot of changes. I'll tell you the truth, it's got so that the laws have got so tight that it's made it hard really to make a living.'

When he started it cost two dollars and seventy-five cents for a licence 'and you could do anything – crab pot, you could net, you could scrape or use bank traps but now you need a licence for anything you do and it costs money. My licence cost me about seventy-five dollars. A young man's licence could cost six hundred or seven hundred dollars. We used to go down to Virginia but it can cost fifteen hundred dollars to go crab in Virginia waters nowadays.

'Crabs go in cycles but I know, when I was coming up a boy, crab used to swim by a lot – we used to have a lot of channel traps – but the last few years I haven't seen that. I suppose there's so many crab pots in the water they keep the crabs out in deep water and they feed on the bait that they put in the crab pots. It used to be when I was a boy we would all go down the crick and wait for the flood tide to start, and we would all line up and catch "swimmers" – as we would call them – swimming by and we'd just dip 'em with our crab net, but that way of life is gone, I supppose crab potting is what changed that too.'

Working the water is a hard way to make a living, beset by the vagaries of the weather, and heavily dependant on the run of luck that fills the bushels with crabs. 'You're your own boss but it's a hit-or-miss existence. Some days you find nothing. Starting of the Second World War, in the early 1940s, the crab got so scarce here that the people just had to leave and went to the city to get defence jobs. My father worked in the shipyard in Baltimore. I've seen it so scarce you can hardly make a living. Right now it's scarce, it's just a trickle, it's an up-and-down job.'

The longest shadow cast over Waverley and his family's lives was the devastating death of his twin brother.

'He was out in the sound one day dredging for oysters, and it was cold and the culling board had ice on it. He was in the cabin getting a cup of coffee and when he came out to pull the dredge in – I mean that's how we understand what happened – he stepped on the ice culling board and slipped and went overboard. He had a few duck traps out in the marsh where it was muddy and sticky and you would have to have your boots on tight, and he would have had so many socks on that he would have had to stomp to get his boots on, and we believe that he couldn't put his boots off which caused him to drown. The water was so cold that the doctor said his heart was chilled. He stayed underwater so long that he exhausted himself . . .'

The death of a brother would be tragedy enough but the fact he was a twin was of course far closer to the bone. 'Man it was hard to adjust. We did everything together. We slept in the same bed until we were eight or nine years old. Yes, we did everything together . . .'

Waverley knows that the skills he employs on the water are things you could only learn by being in the open-air university that is the Bay: you could never learn the things he knows between the covers of a book. He is humble about his art and craft: 'I think it would take you some doing to pick it up by your own. We do things different I guess. Some guys come down from the city – they think they can do things like we do but they have a hard job to adjust to it.'

One example of his adept way of handling a boat is the pace at which one proceeds through the water.

'The speed you go with your boat is to drag your scrapes along. I used to just look over the stern and see the texture of the water, the mud behind and tell you how fast or slow you were going and working the tides – which were good for crabbing and we learn it coming up – how to make do with what we've got – there's no manual on it – we learn from doing, from our own experience.'

The way he spoke about his trade reminded me of the coracle fishermen, who ply their willow and tar boats along the river Tywi back home in Wales, fishing for salmon. The fishermen work in pairs and I remember one old man telling me how his partner could 'listen' to the river. He had merely to dangle his hand in the water and he could tell if the tide was turning at the river mouth or even if there were fish running. One day he woke up and found to his great consternation that he had lost the ability to hear the river in this very special way. As his friend said: 'He had gone deaf in his right hand.'

Boats keep Smith Island's way of life afloat. A recent census revealed 146 workboats, 136 skiffs and seventeen specialised vessels such as ferries, the school boat and pleasure craft. Many watermen have more than one boat. Unlike the rest of the U.S., where the top ten names for boats in 1993 were Serenity, Obsession, Osprey, Fantasea, Liquid Asset, Therapy, Seduction, Happy Hours, Solitude and Wet Dream, the fleet is named after wives, daughters, sisters and mothers – Miss Peggy, Miss Sherry, Darlene and Miss Maxine. These names are permanent, even if a mother or a loved one dies, because it's considered bad luck to change a boat's name hereabouts, just as it's considered taboo to use any blue paint on a workboat. Many were made by hand in the Bay and there is a special Smith Island nomenclature for many of a craft's component parts. What are elsewhere referred to as 'frames' are 'battens' here, 'strongbacks' are 'knees' and there are other localisms such as the planking known as 'deadwood in the deadrise' and the 'dump box' – the boxed-off washboard where the crab scrape is dumped and the contents culled.

There is one verse in a poem by remembrancer Jennings Evans which pretty much sums up the relationship between a waterman and his boat. 'You might say a waterman lives/An unusual way of life/He spends more time with his boat/Than he does with his wife.'

The wind had picked up and beat at the planking of the shanty. But the quiet man still had plenty to say and share so this was time most rewardingly spent. The wind could have kept us there for a week, and Waverley would still have had a repository of recollections to share. As the talk turned to the weather he directed my gaze at his hilarious weather barometer. 'Barometers don't get simpler than this,' he said, grinning impishly. It was little more than a piece of rope hanging on a shelf. Waverley cheerfully explained its *modus operandi*. 'If the rope is moving it's windy. If the rope is still it's calm. If the rope is wet it's raining. If the rope is dry it's sunny. If the rope is white that means it's snowed on it. If the rope is invisible it's foggy. Now if the rope is gone it's a hurricane!'

Waverley has seen harsh weather and hard times but one of the most testing things he has had to cope with has been the perennial decline in the island population, an emptying of the soul of the place.

'When I growed up there was about two hundred and fifty people living on this part of the island; 'course now it's about eighty people or something. There was no trouble to hear children a-hollering but now the state has closed our school and even the children have to go by ferry to Ewell to kindergarten. We've got three or four babies coming along – that's a help.'

The old waterman didn't himself receive much education: '. . . only to ninth grade and that was it. Used to be then the high school was over on the mainland and if anybody went they had to stay there and pay board. The county paid some but not all but I couldn't make it so I had to quit and come home. They used to say that Smith has the only school in Maryland which would be closed not only because of snow but also because of wind.'

The Bay may be be wide and the skies possessed of a certain immensity; but for Waverley the church is the centre of existence. 'To me that's the centre of activity. I see God everywhere I look. God is the creator – everything you see has got life in it and God created it; he put it here for our use or our purpose – it can be misused and a lot of us misuse it. I've done it myself. We never have to sow like the farmer who has to go and buy seed. We get our crab pots ready in the winter and believe that there are going to be crabs in the spring and that God is going to supply our needs.'

73

Sometimes there are epiphanic moments for the men out fishing in the open-air church that is the water – you can hear them whooping with delight and fear and sometimes it is just the lay preachers practising and hollering – 'sometimes they'd get happy right aboard their boat'.

In the winter the wildfowl fly in, not only a thrilling spectacle in themselves, but also an eagerly awaited supplement to the diet. But there are few ducks now. 'It used to be illegal to trap ducks but with us it was a survival thing, catching them in traps baited with corn which we'd buy on the cob and shell them.' Waverley remembers trapping black ducks and sprigtails, also known as pintails.

'I remember lots of geese here. There used to be a store and I remember seeing the whole floor covered with geeses that people had brought in from hunting Canadas.'

Even an environmentalist such as Tom Horton, who has written so eloquently and passionately about island life on Smith, started out with the blood-lust of the hunter coursing through his veins. He used to have a companion called Ackley Tyler, a hunter so determined that, after a knee operation, he would hobble across the marshes on crutches to retrieve a goose he had shot. Horton spent his Christmas vacations with Ackley and they spent their time 'trapping or shooting raccoon, muskrat, geese, ducks and deer, not to mention fish, oysters and soft- and hard-shell crab.'

In any conversation on Smith the subject of crabs is never far away. Our talk turned to the changing fortunes of the blue crab, whose population is so erratic that on a graph it looks like a rollercoaster. Waverley blames rockfish for the troughs. Rockfish numbers increased courtesy of a moratorium for which Waverley thought there was no need – 'for then there got to be so many they're having an effect on crabs.'

'I myself caught one this spring and when I cleaned it it had had thirty-seven little crabs in its stomach. So you take a school of rock – each one eating thirty-seven crabs – that can soon wipe out a population can't it? We believe the rockfish has had a lot to do with it.'

74

The blue crab feeds on smaller fiddler crabs, periwinkles, clams and worms, and isn't averse to the odd foray into cannibalism as it even gorges on its fellow blue crab. In the meadows of the sea, dramas of birth and rebirth, murder, cannibalism and courtship are continually being played out. For the crab's part, this series of events follows a cycle of growth and moult which will end – for the unfortunates – with an encounter with the fishing skills of the likes of Waverley, followed by a midnight truck trip to bustling fish markets such as New York City's Fulton, or even a journey as air-freight to the restaurant tables of Japan.

Waverley's knowledge of crabs is not that of the biologist: his is the knowledge of the instinctive and observant hunter. It is a study of tide and time and of the habits of Cancer. He crabs to earn a living, while fishing is one of his favourite pastimes.

One of his daughters gave him a hat which hangs on a nail on the wall. The motto running across the peak proclaims that he is a proud member of the 'Laid-back Fishermen's Association.'

'The fish has picked up this last couple of years. Hardheads, crokers have come back strong, the spots come back, the perch is come back, the bluefish are on the way back; I caught some this weekend. They got to make a difference – they eat a lot of crab.'

Picked up perhaps, but there was a time when the Chesapeake was almost a byword for abundance, as was recorded by the seventeenth-century observer George Alsop:

As for fish, which dwell in the watery tenements of the deep, here in Maryland is a large sufficiency, and plenty of almost all sorts of Fishes, which live and inhabit within her several Rivers and Creeks, far beyond the apprehending or crediting of those that never saw the same, which with very ease is catched, to the great refreshment of the Inhabitants of the Province.

Even in the late nineteenth century, bragging advertisements would describe the Bay as the Mediterranean Sea of America.

On Tylerton the tapestry of daily life is woven from small motifs and quiet colours. Men gather round the store of an evening – and 'sort of rehearse what happened that day'. Of course the on-board radios are another way to keep up with the gossip but Waverley's CB is very old so he mainly listens.

Some watermen can make a crab fall asleep by rubbing its belly. Waverley has seen it done. 'Rub its belly and it just relaxes. Some people they come in and they say they've got a crab figured out, and the next day the crab does just the opposite of what you've learned. Just when you think you understand a crab it crosses you up. It's a mystery.'

Waverley makes his own pots to catch crabs. 'I guess it takes an hour to make a pot – of course I'm not one of the fast ones. The guys who make a living from it can make one much faster. The wire you use is galvanised wire and you put a frame around it and staple it together and put a weight on it, a rod iron like they use in cement foundations – and then your corks and your lines. I guess they cost fifteen dollars a pot.'

One of the biggest forces for change at Tylerton has been the Chesapeake Bay Foundation, where they've had a 'right many people coming of late'. Waverley doesn't come down too hard on the Foundation. 'We thought they were trying to disrupt our way of life and make things harder on us. They're kind of strict I guess. I'm a conservationist; I don't like to see things wasted. If I go out and catch something I want to use it and eat it – if it's small or big there's no harm in eating it. To go out and catch it just to say you caught it – I don't believe in that at all. Really the fishermen on the television – they make me mad to tell you the truth. They'll go out and catch a big fish and wear it out until it's nearly about dead and bring him in, take the hook out and let him go back in again. They think he's going to live, but nine times out of ten that fish is going to die. That makes me mad. Anybody that goes out and kills something or catches something and don't use it – I don't go along with that.

'A lot of people think that a waterman is out there to devour things and bring it in and catch everything they can, but that's not true. We go out and catch what we need to make a living. So the people don't understand that – they think we're hogs. That's my living and I try to preserve what's out there so I'll have something to go to the next day.

'It's awful dangerous. If you're not careful, sometimes a sea could hit you and throw you off balance and over the side. If there's no one around to see what happened at that moment then you're gone.

'We had a ceremony in the spring of blessing the fleet – the first year we've done it. Jennings had compiled a list of everybody who'd drowned and I think it was about twenty – so that's not too bad; it's rare for a waterman to drown. People come out from the mainland for a weekend and they see a squall coming and they don't realise that anything can come out of a squall on the Bay.'

In John Barth's novel *Once Upon a Time*, ten minutes of just such unexpected weather causes a couple who have left their home on Columbus Day 1999 to plough into the shoals off Smith Island, ten minutes which are 'macho, scary and not undangerous . . . everything heaving and slamming and flailing until finally secured, while the wind batters and the waves pound and the rain strafes.'

That's the sort of heavy weather that Waverley never makes light of. That colourful pioneer John Smith also encountered heavy weather hereabouts, near this archipelago which he christened 'The Isles of Limbo'. He and his men had a tempestuous time there:

> . . . the wind and waters so much increased, with thunder, lightning and rain, that our foremast blew overboard, and such mighty waves overwrought us in that small barge, that with great labour, we kept her from sinking by freeing out the water. Two days were we enforced to inhabit the uninhabited isles; which, for the exception of gusts, thunder, rain, storms and ill weather, we called Limbo.

Waverley underlines the dangers of inclement weather. 'When we see a squall coming we head for the shore –

sometimes a waterspout can come out of it, sometimes a great lot of wind, sometimes a lot of rain and you're caught out in it and it can do damage before you realise it, so many people get caught out. We just respect it and get out of its way.'

I encountered one such squall myself whilst canoeing on what seemed to be a millpond afternoon. Paddling out on open water, a wind came up from nowhere and for twenty minutes I could make no headway. Gradually I was pushed closer and closer to a muddy bank and, despite paddling vigorously, the wind kept me, all seventeen stone of me, pinned in place like a butterfly in a museum display case.

They also get serious winds sweeping across Smith, hurricanes such as Agnes which was enough to change the whole ecology of the Bay, and the likes of Hazel, not just breezing but *really* blowing in.

The Bay is big and Waverley has had to range right across it to eke out a living. 'Some of the watermen range far and wide – as far a hundred miles down to the Bay Bridge Tunnel. In the wintertime we go above the Bay Bridge.'

The year is punctuated by the big Christian festivals, as Waverley tells me:

'Christmas is very special to us – my mother used to put up a tree and decorate, and we used to think the world of a little yard with a little fence with a barn and animals she would set in there and all the animals and nativity scene. She never did put it up until Christmas Eve.

'We never had many toys. I remember once I got a target set – a little pistol with sticker cowboys and Indians. If we could get a pair of boots, man, we thought we were rich! We used to hang up our stockings or lay them out by the tree and she would fill that with oranges and apples and nuts and candy and stuff – man, we thought we had the world! One Christmas she gave us a little switch. I think we've got closer to the essential message of Christmas.'

Waverley's skills seem to know no bounds . . .

'I used be the chief of the fire department, one of the founders of it in the 1960s. Not a huge department. We have

78

pretty good equipment; we have a huge fire engine, much too big for this part of the island. It's hard to manoeuvre on these small roads – we just need a smaller pumping outfit.' He only remembers three bad fires – 'mainly our duties are to the sick'.

The wind blows a little more quietly now, so Wave starts preparing the bait. 'We use alewives – menhaden for bait. I cut them up and bait the pot with them.'

Menhaden is a superabundant fish. Hundreds of millions of tons are landed annually and it has names galore; *pogy* in New England; in the middle Atlantic states it is known as the *mossbunker*; in North Carolina the *fatback*. On the Chesapeake they stick to *menhaden* or *bunker* but on the Eastern shore the name takes on a historical resonance when it is referred to as *alewife* or *old wife*, a name used as far back as the doomed colony established by Sir Walter Raleigh at Roanake.

'I've got my pots in shallow water – in four, five or six foot of water. Most of the other potters are in fifteen, twenty or thirty foot and they have pot-pullers. The sea can hit you and shove the pot under the boat and catch in your wheel. It's backbreaking and monotonous work.'

Waverley used to catch terrapins – recently there had been a moratorium on them – but now there's a different time of year for selling them. Terrapin used to be a popular commodity in the state of Maryland. A man called Louis ran the terrapin industry but now demand has declined. That it used to be a favoured delicacy is a fact attested to by the name of the local basketball team: The Terrapins. 'My daughter made some bank traps – they're three-foot square and you run a hedge into the bank – they catch anything that's crawling along the edge of the bank and they catch a lot of terrapins. When we catch terrapins we just let them go.

'Sea turtles, on the other hand, they can tear up a pot, they're strong. 'Course, I guess all they've got to do is put their weight on one and mash them down so they can tear things up at times. They tell me their main food is sea nettles.'

Waverley adjusts the Smith Island baseball cap on his head. The island used to have a team that played in the Central

Shore league, but the bleachers at Tylerton now are rotten through, the cheers of the crowd no more than thin, imagined echoes drifting in from the past.

With the inevitability of a military general turning a conversation to the subject of tactics, Waverley moved us on, or back to, you guessed it, crabs! 'I love crabs now as well as I ever did. Stewed Jimmies are my favourite. It's the big crab and the way we prepare them. We cut the fins off. We pull the back off and pull the fins – leave the claws on and the body and then we take it home. My wife cleans them with a brush and then she'll put them in the pot and stew 'em down and make gravy and onions and potatoes – Jimmy gravy with a pan of corn bread, and then put the gravy on the corn bread. Man you've never eaten crabs till you've had stewed Jimmies. They're pretty scarce this year.

'Environmentalists try to tell us that it's over-harvesting, over-fishing, but I think that's the least of the problems. They're against us nine times out of ten. A lot of people resent our way of life because they think we're out here making a barrel of money but really we're only just existing. We are an easy target because we haven't the means or the money to fight back.'

A boat costs enough to cripple a man financially. 'A boat nowadays can cost sixty to seventy thousand dollars. It's not easy to jump into a job on the water nowadays.'

On the water. 'I wouldn't know any other way of life. I've been born and raised right here. I wouldn't trade it for any that I know of right now. 'Course, money-wise I'm not wealthy, but I've never been in want either.'

Finally, the wind quietens sufficiently for us to venture onto 'the water'. As he drifts onto his own form of auto-pilot the chop and swell cause us to lurch and plummet but Wave seems oblivious, as happy as a sandboy.

Just as with any job there are good days and there are bad days. 'A good day is when you got a good catch, the weather's cool, there's no sea nettles or gnats or flies to bother you, a cool day. A bad day is when everything goes backwards – not catching anything, hot, a lot of sea nettles around, greenhead flies are biting on you, you're sweating and you come in and you're just worn out.'

Wave took me to a place called Hog Neck Bottom where the clump of trees marks where people used to live. 'It's a shallow place where I've got my pots, and I have to wait for the tide so I can get to them. There seems to be more males on the inside. Cricks are quite good for crabs.'

Wave shows me a place called Shanks where the sea has claimed every bit of what once was land. He is still railing against the iniquities of the ways of the environmentalists . . .

'Seems like nowadays animals are more valuable than human beings.'

Wave works methodically, separating the males from the females, snapping the claws off the peelers which will go in the float so they won't bite on each other. The price for them can be good – 'it got as high as a hundred dollars a bushel in the fish markets'.

He gets five crabs out of one pot. 'A good pot would catch ten or twelve. Only three or four and that's not too good.' The oval entrance to the pot is perfectly designed to allow the crab's flat carapace easy passage into its prison.

One crab attempts a getaway and scuttles across the deck, then hunkers down like a baseball catcher, its mouth bubbling air. Sometimes crabs choose to leave the water, often for several hours – especially during the summer, when they are avoiding seasonal decreases in dissolved oxygen in the water.

'Sometimes your pot gets so full of sea nettles you can hardly lift it. You never get immune to them. They can set you on fire.' White globs of sea nettles cling to the mesh of the pot, shimmering like ectoplasm in the sun. Sea nettles may look like gossamer underwater but they can sting like hornets. Wave uses a lotion called 'Skin So Soft' or fresh water to wash off the nettles.

Waverley points a papier-mâché finger at the water underneath the boat. 'The sea grass is gone. It used to be one of the choice crabbing bottoms in the Bay, used to be grass shore to shore.' As the boat moves in towards the state line Waverley points out one of the distinctions between the genders of crabs. Female underparts look like the domed outline of the Capitol building while the male most resembles the phallic shape of the Washington monument.

'We do find more crabs in the pots near the state line,' states Waverley with an impish grin. It's not a catch to write home about but there do seem to be more skirting the line. If truth be told most of the crabs are the other side of the line. This seems to have more than just a grain of truth as there are eight in the pot which has drifted just under the marker for the state divide.

Years before, they had fights over the state line. It is not unheard of for a crabber to drag the buoys that mark the state divide a few hundred feet quite by accident, an act of bloodless annexation which can put a few more crabs within reach.

We then checked out some bank traps. He looks at them every other day. 'In the spring then they're the best – that's when they do best. What you do catch is nice pretty crabs – that's the reason I keep them out really.'

Gradually, crab by crab, the bushel filled up. They fitted snugly on top of each other, benthic warriors with their claws akimbo. The cerulean sky above was a broken line of milky clouds. The ninety horsepower Mercury outboard motor drove us on over underwater grasses that drifted with the current.

We were trailed by a row of gluttonous gulls. Expectant and hungry, their sharp eyes followed every movement of Waverley's wiry hands, mesmerised as he set up the necessary rhythm to pull up the pot from its bed. He manoeuvred the boat to the next pot even as he sorted out the catch in a wooden box.

'Sometimes the wind makes it awful hard to get to your pot,' he said. Waverley's pots are marked by purple corks with orange tops. The tide wasn't very high and the propeller occasionally churned up the channel mud into clouds of grey silt.

A fish crow flew past up above, a small speck against the sun. Wave arched his back with a groan as he hauled the last pot on board his small craft.

'Just about everybody suffers with a bad back. I'm nearly dead, can't straighten up.'

We retired for breakfast. This endearing old man proudly fixed me up with his speciality. A Waverleyburger involves compressing some eggs between two doorstop slices of bread.

We also enjoyed some of his wife Ruth's fig preserve – figs, pears and pomegranates grow easily in the island soil – but this year Waverley thinks the figs are dry. Waverley loves his figs – he usually gets through a pint of them a week.

His wife came in after a stint of crab processing. Like her husband she had been up since four o' clock in the morning. She admitted she's getting a little bit slow when it comes to the business of crab-picking, having only managed eleven or twelve pounds – the other lady with her was twice as fast.

Ruth collects apples. Their house is a veritable orchard. She has a dinner bell in the shape of an apple. There are red, carved apples arrayed on shelves and, most charmingly, a tiny apple-shaped house on tiny legs which turns out to be a mosquito house.

They both like to get up to New York to see a winter show. He supports the New York Yankees and the Baltimore Orioles. I tried to imagine the old couple negotiating subways and dwarfed by skyscrapers. This is their habitat, this island enclosed by waves.

Apologetically, *sotto voce*, she says of her husband that he is known to be a quiet man, that you wouldn't know he was in the room. Me, I found The Quiet Man positively loquacious.

Chapter 8

THE BLEAK SEASON

Now the ice lays its smooth claws on the sill,
The sun looks from the hill
Helmed in his winter casket.
And sweeps his arctic sword across the sky.

Edwin Muir, 'Scotland's Winter'

Waverley Evans told me how the past four or five years had seen fairly decent winters. But there have been chill periods which have paralysed island life. 'One year we were froze in for three or four days. Ice cutters have to be used to get into us and bring in supplies during hard winters. In 1976 we were froze in solid for about six weeks, and the only thing that was coming back and forth then was military helicopters. They flew in supplies like oil, and then they would carry people over to the mainland to get groceries.'

Elmer Evans's memory is long enough to remember the Great Winter of 1936. 'I was nine or ten years old that year. I used to live across this little crick where all the houses are all gone now. I remember when the whole community used to get out on the ice and build a big bonfire and we would just skate around and people would bring out rocking chairs and they would push them round on the ice. A cub plane with skis on it was piloted by a man called Al Bennett who would take people off who were sick or needed hospitalisation. A man called Stitts came in with a two-winger aeroplane – he landed across the crick to pick up Mrs Lena Tyler and he had just time to get her off before the ice started breaking up again.'

This is the season when an airborne metronome beats out its rhythm as the tundra swans wing in from northern climes to winter in the Chesapeake. You can hear the swish of cold air displaced by the flapping of their strong wings, and you see their long necks outstretched as they survey the winterlands beneath.

In his book, *Snowfall*, Tom Horton tells of how the 'hubbub of swans in a flock forced down by fog on to the Allegheny river were voices that of course, brought police swarming, sure that a horrible riot was in progress.' But on the water, swans are the very essence of elegance. You may have an exultation of larks, or a spring of teal, but with swans, well you surely have a serenity, yes a serenity of swans.

The land of pleasant living is how the beer commercials described the Chesapeake, yet when the wind whips up the biting salt spray, and you're a long way from home, the crabber-turned-winter-oysterman has anything but a pleasant living.

For in the Chesapeake, some crabbers forsake the crabs, as the thermometer drops, or sometimes plummets, and turn their attention to oysters.

Oyster dredging came to the Chesapeake in the 1820s when the stocks ran low in Connecticut and New England, whose watermen drifted south to scour the plentiful beds off the Maryland coast. The triangular steel frames of the dredges scraped the bottoms, and the oysters were gathered in a rope-and-chain bag connected to the rear of the scrape. The local populace was incensed by this foreign harvesting of their waters, and passed a succession of laws, firstly forbidding the use of dredges, then allowing them, then changing their minds and allowing only native Marylanders to use them. Some watermen moved from the North and came to live within sight of the abundant submarine banks. Dredging was hard and dangerous. Vicious and voracious captains were hard-pressed to find willing workers, and consequently many crew members were shanghaied after a hard session's drinking in Baltimore bars. Locked into their cabins at night, they lived in fear for their lives by day, especially at the end of the season when a captain knew full well that he didn't have to pay a man who'd been washed overboard because of an accident.

Oyster dredgers had violent run-ins with those who tonged for the molluscs. Tonging involves using a pair of metal claws which clamp together just like the jaws of an earth-moving excavator. Others simply flew in the face of new regulations which had been introduced to try to establish some semblance of control. This piratical period led to the formation of the Maryland Oyster Navy who had to police waters riven by disputes, which sometimes had to be settled by the use of naval howitzers!

Most Smith islanders agree that oystering is getting harder because of a sharp decrease in numbers. Dr. Roger Newell of the University of Maryland's Horn Point Environmental Laboratory has offered the staggering estimate that there used to be sufficient oysters in the Bay before 1870 to filter the entire volume of water in the Chesapeake, all eighteen trillion gallons of it, every few days. Molluscs even give their names to towns on the shore, such as Bivalve, Maryland and Oyster, Virginia. Nowadays the techniques for gathering oysters are changing, and divers account for a fifth of the Chesapeake catch. They can see and harvest the molluscs rather than relying on the pot-luck approach of the oyster dredger.

Jennings Evans has pored over a mass of old newspapers and documents to discover that there has been a string of very hard winters on Smith: in 1780, 1832, 1864, 1868, 1895, 1917, 1927, 1936 and 1977. Ice packed in the islands up to twenty inches thick, and the ice was usually presaged by stupendous snowfalls with drifts sometimes reaching the second storeys of the island homes, although some were mercifully only waist high.

Elmer Evans's store of winter memories goes way, way back: 'Holland Island where I was born, well, in 1918 it was a bad winter. The doctor came right over the fences in a horse and sleigh there to Black Walnut Point. They had one piece of flatback – pork belly – they passed it from one family to another. One family used black-eyed beans and ruined the flatback and they threatened to string 'em up – string up the whole family that ruined the flatback.'

One of the most interesting stories discovered by Jennings concerns one William Saulsbury who, during one of the earliest recorded freeze-ups in 1780, jilted the woman he was going to marry. She promptly cursed him. His personality changed instantly – as so often happens with efficient curses – but there was worse to come. One afternoon, he and his companion Job Parks Jr. went duck hunting. Returning with a good bag, Saulsbury, also carrying the weight of his curse, fell into an ice hole and by morning he was dead. Picks and shovels had to be used to break the ground for his coffin, and after he was buried 'a flame of fire was seen lingering over his grave, where it remained glowing through the winter nights, in plain view of the islanders who shudderingly regarded it in association with the curse that was placed on him by his former fiancée'.

Terrible winters and tragedies have followed. In the ice-hard winter of 1936, for example, a dramatic attempt was made to bring supplies to Smith across the frozen wastes of Tangier Sound. A fifteen-man expedition, led by Major Enoch Carey, had to be rescued, with all the members suffering from exhaustion and exposure. One man, Sergeant W.V. Hunter, perished in the attempt.

Ben Whitney remembers icebergs. 'In 1977 we had icebergs out here – tall icebergs.' He talks about them with a certain relish and in the mind's eye I can see them, conical witches' hats made of glass, silently scything through chill water.

But winter is a time of miracles too, as Mayberry Marsh knows:

'I think around Christmas the men couldn't get through Chesapeake Bay to the island, as all this ice had formed out there, and this good old woman she had a lot of faith – she prayed, she said "Lord, let our men get home," she said, "let the ice break up so they can get home," and sure enough it began to break up a little bit at a time, and kept on until a way opened and they all got home. So you know the Lord heard that prayer – and then after they all got here it closed back up.'

Chapter 9

SPINESHIVERY STORIES

It was a fearful page in the record of my existence, written all over with dim, and hideous, and unintelligible recollections.

Edgar Allen Poe, *Berenice*

One can imagine how things were when, with winter lashing the island, the people would gather to swap yarns, and in particular ghost tales designed to raise goosebumps and send an icy shiver down the spine. Faces would be lit up by the flickering lights of the candles. The wind would howl like a banshee in the eaves. And now the year's shadows have lengthened and little remains of the day – a few brief hours of wan light and then plenty of time to scare each other witless!

Smith Island is both religious and superstitious at one and the same time. Watermen don't take chicken in their bail or lunch boxes as they believe that doing so would be enough to bring about instant disaster. Women feel the same about anything blue. A poor fellow who went to buy a blue wheelbarrow ended up paying an extra ten dollars to paint her a different colour. Catching a shoe instead of a crab is thought to be a sign of good luck, and when some people bait a crab pot they kiss the pot in the hope of a good catch that day.

Stories with a supernatural edge abound on Smith. Take, for example, the story about a young boy, Solomon Marshall, who was out walking along the bank of a creek one day, minding his own business, when a pirate appeared from nowhere and said to him, 'Come with me and I'll give you a whole lot of gold.' After that unexpected encounter the boy went home and became deranged, simply because he'd seen a ghost. The gold weighed the same as a man's sanity.

Ben Whitney, of Rhodes Point, had a tale for me, too:

'The house I used to live in was near the Mack, the community centre. I'd bang on the stair door and hear the craziest noise up there that I ever heard in my life – just like somebody tearing something up. I'd go upstairs afterwards – you couldn't see nothing. I was scared to sleep up there. One night I went into the kitchen and I heard the greatest slam banging in this kitchen. I went in there about eleven o'clock; I was getting ready to go to bed. I said, "God what was that?" Then there were three knocks. I thought somebody was going to tear my door off – I looked out there; couldn't see a soul. I thought God, leave the door, they were tearing it up! A preacher similarly heard three knocks on the door and went to look outside only to find nobody there. A day later there were some more knocks on the door. On the third day there was somebody at the door, there to tell him somebody was dead. He'd been given a warning that somebody was going to die.'

Elmer Evans, in the meantime, had a close encounter with a big man in the dark:

'I come home one night – Buster Evans had a store and it had a movie house – I seen this big tall fella standing there right where you turn to come into my yard – and I couldn't make him out, only he was all black and tall. I didn't know anybody on Smith Island as tall as he is, and he turned and started walking off. He was going to have to pass through the light up there from the back of Bus's store, 'cause that's showing on the road up there and I'll see who that is. He never did pass through that light and I never did see him again, but I believe he's at least seven foot tall.'

'Another time, not too many years ago, I was trotlining. I saw this skiff painted red and the only one who had a copper-coloured skiff was called Jimmy "Rar" Evans. I ran my trotline out and he was gone. Where in the world had he disappeared to all in a sudden?'

All Hallows' Eve can bring out the bogey man in the best of us, and the people of Smith are no exception. There are many stories such as the one about the woman in white whose apparition haunts the road near the old coffin-house, or the man who saw the snake with saucer-eyes near the old Pitchcroft house, or the ghost down by the Waiting Place bridge that 'didn't have no head'. One can imagine the children, their eyes round with fear, their little hearts racing, hanging on to every frightening word, as they hear of a herd of headless horses that cantered over Wading Place Bridge, or a spectral baby that wailed in the marsh.

Stella Bruce has a ghost yarn or three in her:

'As a girl I used to love to hear the older people telling what we called ghost yarns. Before my mother and father was married they lived way over there. My father, he had to cross three bridges over the guts between here and there. Anyway, he had been over to see my mother one night – he was on his way back home we didn't have no electric then, and no lights you know, and it was real dark, and anyway he went to jump off a bridge onto the road that was there, and there was this big dog – my father was a truthful man; I don't believe he ever told a lie in his life – he said that dog had eyes as big as saucers and he would go on the other side of the road and try to pass the dog and he couldn't pass it. So then he jumped to the other side and the dog would jump right in front of him every time so he didn't know what to do so he kicked at it and it vanished. My father said the hair stood right up on his head!

'Another time he had a big boat that you could put oysters in, and there was two men that went with him. They were tied up alongside the wharf over there at Crisfield. That night, the two men he had aboard with him, they were all down in the cabin and they were asleep and he was a-sitting there. By and by he heard something buzzing, and he said the first thing you know it was just like a horse and cart had backed up to that boat and had dumped out a whole cartload of chains on her, and she even walled out – that's when the waves come up the boat – and anyway he said, "I don't want to hear this by myself; I'm going to wake Coley and Shafter," – that's what their names were. Anyway, they woke up and he told them to listen, but by then a blizzard had started and the same thing happened. Well, you know, there was a drawbridge close there, and that next morning they heard about this man and woman was a-going across the drawbridge, and it was open, and they went down and they both got drowned. One of them was black and one was white – I don't know which was the female. Anyway, they pulled the car up right across his deck so that was a sign that that was going to happen.'

Other stories on Smith derive from the character of Brit the witch who really had the look of a witch straight out of a story by the Brothers Grimm – with a long nose to match long dirty fingernails.

Mayberry Marsh has a story which tells of an eerie premonition:

'One of my great-uncles, he was coming over here – you know the men all used to meet at the store of an evening – after they'd get their work done they'd all gather and talk about things. He was going by a house on his way home, and it was an elderly man who lived there, and he was on his deathbed, and when he went by there a woman in black brushed past him. The next night she did the same thing, then the third night he had to pull right away to keep her from brushing him on his arm, and the next morning that man was dead, so I guess that was a sign of his death. And they're all truthful people.'

They are that.

Chapter 10

GRAVE ENQUIRIES

Names illegible beneath layered moss
Clip me to futility, yet give that mild
Pleasure we feel in cemeteries . . .

John Tripp, 'At Bosherston Ponds'

Gail Wolczyck, an accountant from Long Island, has bought a house on Smith, where she spends as much time as possible diligently following the roots of her lineage. This has been her labour and delight these past twenty years, which she has spent tracing ancestors, tracking down dusty documents and visiting haunting graveyards. I met her in the graveyard outside Tylerton church, where she helped to decode the stories encapsulated in the headstone inscriptions.

The graveyard at Ewell is so full of Evanses that it could be a private cemetery. The ranks of stone mark not just a long lineage extending back through the fog of the centuries but give glimpses too, of a larger history, redolent of events far beyond the island's shores. Thus there are many Benjamin Franklins, George Washingtons and Thomas Jeffersons. There are many Wesleys named in honour of John Wesley and even some girls were given Wesley as a middle name – as a tribute to the man who established the Methodist church.

The well-kept headstones of the island's cemeteries, with lawns manicured to the smooth greenness of a billiard table, offer ample evidence of the respect people of Smith feel for their forebears.

There are nicknames galore such as Sug, Johnny Biscuit, Dink, Woods and Wicks, as well as names that could only derive from far-off times. In the 1700s and 1800s, children were named after biblical figures like Josiah, 'fire of the Lord', Kiturah which means 'burned offering', or Zipporah, 'a bird'.

In the 1900s it was not uncommon to name a child after the local doctor. Many were named after one Dr. Charles Gladstone.

There are Greek and Latin names too – Euphemia meaning good speech, and Triphenia, meaning delicate.

Spelling wasn't as formalised then as it is now, and the clerks of the courts, the ministers, the census-takers and even the stonecutters wrote down names as they heard or misheard them – so Parthannia, Greek for virgin, became Bothanna; Britannia was corrupted to Britann; and Keziah, a Hebrew name meaning fragrant, became Kissy. There are many abbreviations and alterations – Matadora became Dora, Temperance became Tempy, Permelia evolved to Milly, Sophonia to Flora, Trephenia to Triffy, Zipporah to Zippy, Cornelia to Neely, Anastasia to Stace, Elpertina to Teenie, Teener or Teen, and Sedonia to Dona or Donie.

Gail started our grand tour of the graveyard at an iron tombstone – 'This is Butler Tyler – great-grandson of the first Tyler on the island who owned most of Tylerton. He died about 1824. On top of here is a baby who died 6 November 1825 – probably the great niece of Butler Tyler who only had daughters.'

'All three cemeteries on Smith Island were family plots, not church cemeteries. People used to be buried probably someplace on the farm and away from the house, though not more than thirty feet because of the problems with Indians who, paradoxically, respected cemeteries – not that there were many Indians.'

There are a good many children's graves on Smith – one has the simple inscription 'Tread lightly, a dream lies sleeping there.' This is a loose derivation from W.B. Yeats' poem 'He Wishes For The Cloths of Heaven' which closes with the lines 'But I being poor, have only my dreams; /I have spread my dreams under your feet; /Tread softly because you tread on my dreams.'

Gail pointed out some of the peculiar features of island burial. 'These are raised graves – that's the original way they would bury – none of the people here are six foot under. If you took the sod off you'd find a brick coffin holder so that the stones like this one here – if you hit it with a finder or a probe you would hear something hard.'

Some island cemeteries are missing, the land having been claimed back by the sea. 'You often find single headstones out in the marshlands. Like over at Francis Gut where people lived until 1933. The people moved off after a big wind, a no-name storm which was probably a hurricane but this was before they called them such.'

There is ample evidence of people dying young. 'We had half the population dying before the age of ten, after that the next big group was women of child-bearing age, then if you get past that the majority lived to sixty-five – barring accidents like drowning or epidemics.

'There's this big jigsaw puzzle and I'm a part of it. Prior to 1860, my family lived here on Horse Hammock on the Virginia Maryland state line. This was in the time of the tall ships when banana barques and the like came up the Bay en route for Baltimore, and some of them would stop at the store. This was the time that gave rise to a rusty tale about Marmaduke Mister's buried treasure, rumours abounding about the amount of gold that sank with him but they were probably nails.' Might this be the pirate who appeared to the young boy who then promptly lost his marbles?

We looked for and found Richard Bradshaw, the oldest stone in Tylerton churchyard. 'He was the first Bradshaw living on Tyler land in 1770, and we think his wife is Arabella Tyler. The first three principal families were Evanses, Tylers and Parkes – there are no more Parkes apart from the ones who came back from away. There were twelve to fifteen Evanses coming into Jamestown between 1607 and 1630, and I've got the list of boats they came in on. I can take the Evans family back to a John Evans born in 1660 who bought land over here, and he had land in Accomack County where he is buried. His

94

sons Mark and John get a goodly part of land on Smith – Mark trades his Smith Island for all the Accomack so John ends up with all the land on Smith.'

Some headstones are decorated with symbols. There is one that Gail claimed as a sign that the grave's incumbent was a Mason although Jennings Evans disagrees with her on just this one point.

We then moved on to willow symbology. 'The willow tree is a very common symbol on a tombstone for the area, sometimes with a single leaf falling. There's sometimes a boat showing that someone has drowned, and often a rose.' Similarly a pyramid marks the death by drowning of a waterman. 'The most recent was an eighteen-year-old boy who had just graduated from high school. There was a boating accident and you can tell from the stone it was recent because it depicts a modern outboard engine.'

Some stones mark the position of the person's foot, a footstone to match the headstone. 'This cemetery is running out of space,' Gail tells me. In the middle of the cemetery is a dead tree with virginia creeper and a mulberry bush growing out of it. The tree, probably an old gum tree, is engulfing a stone – with a diameter of five feet.

How are people buried on Smith? 'When somebody dies they take the body to the Bradshaw's funeral house – they used to have a home at Ewell. The deceased used to be laid out at home, and if it was a case of the person dying of something contagious they might be laid in the ground the same day. Tuberculosis used to be a big killer, as was scrofula or the king's evil, which gets into the bones. They never had an epidemic of TB, but they've had outbreaks of Asian cholera – not child cholera – and dyphtheria.'

One of the pitfalls and dangers for a genealogist comes with the variations of spelling found on birth, marriage and death certificates. 'Registrars didn't spell names properly – Bradshaw became Bradclaw. Even something as simple as Evans ends up being Evins or Evens. First names are destroyed and they also used nicknames – even on the gravestones.'

'Some names show where islanders have travelled; you have Dallas Bradshaw and others called Houston and Austin. In the 1860s, some people went to build roads and cities in the Lone Star State, but came back because of a yellow fever epidemic, and brought the names of the cities with them. The 1870s found a good few Indianas and Missouris being christened, while some names hark back to the distant past such as Christopher Columbus Marsh. It can be mind-boggling for the locals, especially when you tell them you've got fifty-three John Evanses.

'The island has long been an intimate mix – many people did marry their own cousins. My great-great-grandfather John W. Marsh married a woman who was by then Margaret Evans. Her father was Peter Evans, his father was Richard Evans and his mother was Rachel Evans, who married Richard Evans. Now, Rachel's mother was Ephemia, who married Thomas Evans, so I've been what we call "falling back into yourself" – all of a sudden all of my names are the same.'

Chapter 11

THE DELIGHTFUL LADIES

There is no road leading to Tylerton, although the possibility of a land bridge has been mooted from time to time. The town is cut off from Ewell and from the rest of Smith, and it's known by some as the shantytown Venice, a town hemmed in by water on three sides with only seventy-five acres or so of solid ground.

There are six small roads – Bayberry Drive, Tuff Street, Bugeye Road – named after the distinctive Chesapeake boat, – Center Street, Marshall Street and Wharf Road, although civil defence has given them different names – Center Street, Back Road, Shore Road and Cemetery Road.

Stella Bruce's house is on Center Street. It has a solitary air about it, and she welcomed me in as if I were her grandson. She was happy to talk and eager to explain about this and that, and she had invited her friend Mayberry Marsh to join us.

'I'm Stella Bruce. I'm eighty years old and I'm glad I lived to be this old. I was born on Smith. I lived on the other side of the harbour and it was ten of us lived over there. You see, my mother died when I was eleven years of age. She died on my brother's sixth birthday of a brain tumour. Well, my grandfather and grandmother, they moved in with us and helped take care of us – and my aunt and uncle and their family. There was ten of us altogether that lived in that home – in The Ridge we called it.

'We played a lot. I couldn't always come over on this side of the crick – I guess I was afraid I might fall overboard, you know, be drowned or something. Anyway, when I'd ask my grandmother if I could come over and play with some of the girls over on this side, she would say, "no, you can't go and that's the word with the wall on it," – when they said, that you knew you couldn't go.

'I had a nice childhood . . . we played hopscotch and the boys they played marbles and we used to play ball at school; we called it dodge ball – it was a big ball and you'd get in this ring, you know, and see if you could hit somebody with this ball.

'Now, when we used to go up to camp meeting – they had the Tabernacle up at Ewell – my grandmother had a tent up there but you see they got burned down. When I was younger, we used to move up there and they'd have Bible School and we'd learn a lot of old choruses and all there – and they taught us about the Books of the Bible – Genesis, Exodus, Leviticus, Numbers, Deuteronomy, Joshua, Judges, Ruth, Samuel one and two . . . The Bible is very important – that's the backbone of the island – our religion, I would say. We don't have too many young people down here to go to church. We don't even have a school down here because there's not enough small children to have a school open.'

Stella met her husband 'when his father had moved over to Dalton, Virginia – that's a naval proving ground over on the Western shore on the Potomac river, down below Washington D.C., and they came over here on a trip one time, we met, and from then on we knew we were in love. We were a little bit of relation – my mother and his father were cousins – there's a lot of that on here. My mother's mother was a Marshall and there was a lot of Marshalls on here, and a man called John Taffy was the father of these three boys – Pete Marshall, Billy Marshall – he was my great-grandfather and West or Wesley Marshall and most of the children around here were some relation. They used to call us Old Man Taffy's kin – yes, there's a lot of Old Man Taffy's kin around here.

'My husband was a waterman. He crabbed, he didn't do much fishing. He used to scrape, and before he died he potted.

'We all worked hard. I had to work hard when my mother died in 1929. We didn't have washing machines in them days, and I started scrubbing clothes on a board for six people – me, my father, two brothers, and my grandmother and grandfather. That's the reason I wore myself out – I don't have much get up and go now. And then my husband got our own shanty to shed

98

his crabs, and I would let him and my sons go crabbing in their boats, and I would go to the shanty way before dawn and go out into the pound. They didn't have crab floats like they do now, right close to the shanties. We had to go out to floats which were tied to stobs – poles in water – and take the shanty boat out to to dip the crabs – to take the crabs out. This was in the 1960s.'

Stella has seen the population dwindle – it had halved in the past twenty years – and there are only some seventy inhabitants left in Tylerton today. There is a photograph hanging in the Drum Point store which dates from 1974 depicting what was then the new elementary school, an image that once graced the cover of the *Baltimore Sun*. Of the nine boys smiling out at you from the photograph, seven have left the island. The school is now closed, and with that closure, as April Tyler – who rang the bell for the last time in 1996 – said, 'part of the heart of the community has stopped pumping.'

Stella says that being a waterman's wife could be vexing. 'We used to worry a lot, and we knew they were across the Bay, and we knew they were coming over. My grandmother, she could look out at the crick – the creek we call it crick – and she'd be looking out the window: she'd raise her glasses and look out there, and my aunt Virginia would say, "ma, what are you worrying about?" She'd say. "They ought to be getting here now," and say, "Why worry when you can pray?", and she'd say, "Well, I do a little of both." She worried and prayed both.

'We used to have four or five stores here and now we only have that one – for a time we didn't even have any; we used to get all our things from Crisfield. We're a close community – like we're all one family – when one family's in trouble we're all in trouble. We help each other out.

'I'm the organist at the church; I enjoy that and so I guess I'll play until I die – as long as they want me to. It takes longer and longer for me to get warmed up.'

Stella sat at the organ to demonstrate. The instrument exhaled wheezy notes. Stella plays the organ every day. She took lessons from her aunt for about a year and then followed

Leroy Abernethy's correspondence course. She played me snatches of songs in her Top Twenty: *Mack the Knife, The Sheik of Araby, Take me out the Ballgame.*

'We used to play "Rook" of a night,' she says. 'It's a card game, not them playing cards – they had numbers on them and we played Parchizi – it's a board unfolded. You throw dice; each player had four little discs made out of wood, and you take a step at a time depending on how many are on the dice that you throw.

'Now, when I was young our neighbours, you know, they'd gather together at night – it was an elderly man and woman that lived not too far from us – they would come over of an evening and sit there with my grandmother and aunt and all of us, and he would tell some stories about when he used to work on a railroad – they called them shippies – he came here on a boat or something – in them days they would hire people and if they didn't have any home to go to they would come and stay with them and work for their keep, you know, and he was one of them, and anyway this lady, Miss Lee, they got married but they never did have any children. I used to enjoy hearing him spin yarns. We didn't have any electric lights; we had lamps that burned oil and that's how we could see. Now it's like I'm living in a different world since I was young. My scenery's changed and my neighbours have changed.

'When I was a little girl I went over to Long Branch – that's a place way over there where my grandmother used to live (I used to call her Ma Venie) every chance I got. I used to play with Ruth Clayton and Verna Lowe, and sometimes Mayberry and Agnes Dize. As I walked through the door I headed straight for the pantry, and I would say Ma Weenie I'm starving – I couldn't say Ma Venie I'd say Ma Weenie. She usually had homemade ginger snaps and her pantry always smelled real nuggy – smelled good. I played with Ann and Norma and Mabel too; they lived closer to me. After mamma died, Ma Venie and Pa Jessie and Aunt Virginia and her family came to live with us over in Johntown. It was real hard times; we thought we were rich to get an egg to spend for a pennyworth of candy.

100

Sometimes on a Saturday Ma Venie would say, "Do you want a nickel to spend or do you want me to make some taffy?" We'd settle for the taffy – we thought we would get more of that. There were five of us children – Waverley, Weldon, Junior and James and me – they're all dead now except Waverley and me. A man called Captain Mitchell used to buy junk and most of the children here would go junking on Saturdays to make a little spending-change – looking for jar lids and anything copper. We'd go round the puncheons – the bulwarks – when the tide was low to see what we could find.

'Everybody had outside toilets and our toilet paper was catalogues and newspapers.' One of the euphemisms for toilet on Smith is a necessary. 'Our necessary was over the puncheons. We didn't have any toilet tissue, Kleenex or paper towels. I didn't know you could buy them until long after I was married.

'I got married in 1936. We didn't have any oil stoves to leave burning at night – just a wood stove, a King heater, and that would burn out a little while after we went to bed. We got up in the morning to a cold house. Everything would be frozen; we had to thaw water to make coffee. We didn't have washing machines; we had to scrub on the washboard. I had to stay home from school to wash. I didn't have any permanents to make my hair curly until I was sixteen or seventeen. We rolled our hair up on wax paper – instead of plastic they used to wrap bread in such paper and cut up brown paper bags, and sometimes we would use curling irons. Now and then our hair would get scorched. We girls didn't wear pants; we wore dresses with long drawers and cotton ribbed stockings pulled up over them. You had to furl the drawers over so you could pull the stockings up over them – real sexy! In warm weather our underwear was home-made of unbleached muslin; the top, which was called a drawer body, had buttons, and the drawers had buttonholes. We had a tank to catch rainwater from the roof – it was awful – almost as bad as a dose of salts – Epsom salts.

'Around Eastertime the whole school would go over in the Pines – that's over thataway, and have an Easter egg hunt.

101

'Sunday nights Mabel and I and our dates would sit in the living room and in those days bedtime was ten o'clock, and courtship often lasted three years.'

Stella's friend Mayberry Marsh arrived: she had marshalled her recollections, because she started on them straightaway.

'Mayberry Marsh – they say it's a southern name. We used to play Annie Overbury – we were supposed to have a ball but our people way back then didn't have much money to spend, and they'd get old stockings and stuff them with rags. You'd have two groups, you know, six on one side of the house and the other group on the other side, and they'd holler "Annie Overbury" – which meant that they were going to throw this thing over – and you were supposed to run around on their side, and they run on your side but if they caught you then you had to get out of the game. Then in the wintertime we used to skate on the ice. We don't have them freezers like we used to.

'I think, but I'm not sure, that I was visited by an angel two years ago. It was a snow blizzard in Crisfield, snowing and blowing, and I had a dog tooth pulled, and all that was on the boat was three head. Anyway the captain could hardly see it was so thick of snowing, and his wife had to get out with a rag and keep that windshield clear. Anyway, we got behind another boat which had radar and transferred, and I got my tooth pulled, and I was coming out of the office onto the main street there, and a woman come alongside of me and put her arm in mine and she never said a word. I had my handbag and my cane and I didn't get a good look at her. I said I'm going down to this senior citizens' place to wait for my boat and ne'er a word – she never said a word. Well we kept walking, it wasn't too far and by and by we got there, and she went and she never said a word.

'When I come home my sister was living then and she said that sounded like an angel. I believe in angels – I read Billy Graham's book – they come to people's assistance: "He will give his angels charge over you to keep you in all your ways."'

The islanders believe in the Devil as well. Mayberry quotes the Book of Isaiah on the subject of Satan being kicked out of Heaven, 'him and his angels. People on the island have had death experiences and seen the devil; they were almost dead and they'd see the devil; they were sinners and they saw him.'

During my stay on the island I heard about one woman who had recently been possessed by demons and, despite her small stature, had managed to hurl a burly guard around a cell in a correctional facility.

'My mother died,' Mayberry continued, 'and left four little girls and we'd come home for lunch from school and we wouldn't have no lunch. Our mother was dead and our father was away oystering; yeah, it was kinda hard.'

Stella and Mayberry discussed the differences between the three towns of Smith. 'Mayberry, I don't want to boast or brag, but many visitors say that people on Tylerton are more outgoing and they show their affection more and are friendly. We had a doctor here at one time, and him and his wife said at Ewell the people were always trying to get ahead of each other – making money, or getting furniture, getting a new car.'

When they talked about Ewell they made it sound like a big city, a real metropolis.

'There used to be telephones on the island but the system wasn't connected to the mainland for a few years. You don't need a telephone – you just go the post office or the picking place to find the news.'

The two remember big community suppers, 'down in the basement, everybody would come and bring pies and cooked chickens and geese – them days we could cook wildfowl, they could catch them – they can't do it now. They were good because they fed them corn.' Stella's father used to have a great big gun.

'Breech loaders,' offered Mayberry, with a husky laugh.

'It's up in the Smithsonian Institute right now,' continued Stella. 'He used to take parties out and they'd skiff up on 'em – they had these running skiffs that would hold this big gun, almost as long as the skiff they were in, and they'd lay there low until all them geese got down and they'd kill maybe as many as fifty a night – Canadas, pintails (we call them sprigtails) – mallards, black ducks, brants and redheads and some teals – they were little. You see they had what they'd call duck traps made out of wire and they had little doors, and once they got inside the door to get at the corn they were trapped, and the door would drop down. My father would get twenty-five ducks at one trap. You got five cents for a pair for picking them. But money was scarce and we used the feathers – shipped them to New York in bags.'

The two have travelled beyond the confines of the island's contours. Between them they have been to Canada, West Virginia and Washington D.C.; Mayberry was in Washington when the King and Queen of England visited in 1939, 'and I saw 'em and I was close by President Roosevelt.'

Neither of them could live for long in cities. Stella lived in Baltimore for a while when her husband worked in Bethlehem steel, in the shipyards. Mayberry has just visited cities – that suits her. They talk across each other about island life. They like 'the freedom; you're your own boss.' 'We can go to bed of a night and not worry – leave our door unlocked – it's peace of mind I think. And then there's the friendliness: if one gets sick the other one helps them out, and if you go to a hospital your neighbours will bring you platters of everything – good things to eat.'

Religion has changed. 'The young people don't respect the Sabbath like our forefathers did – we couldn't go a-boatriding on Sunday – you know, we wouldn't be allowed to play with the scissors on a Sunday. Now they have them right in the church for the children to cut things up.'

Outside the window a symphony orchestra of nocturnal insects was tuning up. The heat, muffled sound and general aura of lassitude attracted the old people to their rocking chairs, and invited the island's cats to dream of slow mice. Mayberry and Stella continued to flip mentally over the calendar years, sepia-coloured ones, pages crinkled at the edges from the touch of too many fingers.

'They were strict, the old people. They were good people though – what they told you you could count on. Take Grandpa Ben – Benjamin Marsh – he sold a boat to somebody down to Tangiers, and that man told him he'd be up on Smith to pay him on such and such a date. Well, anyway, when that date rolled around, he told his Grandma Shadey to get a good dinner ready because that man from Tangier is to be up here today to pay me for that boat. They knewed that they could take each other's word in them days. So anyway, it wasn't long – they got his dinner ready and here he come and he paid him. That's how they were.'

Sometimes, though, the older generation revealed a cruel streak. 'They pretended that they were going to hang Nigger Woods. He stole something and my grandfather was going to hang him. "Captain Ben, I'll never steal anything no more, he said."'

We discussed the fact that Tangier had just refused, on moral grounds, to allow a Mel Gibson movie to be shot on the island, even though it meant that some of the people in the tourist trade would lose out. Mayberry started railing against the skimpy bathing wear that's started to make a provocative appearance around the place. 'They call them thongs – like bikinis but less – their whole cheeks are showing. I'd like to come along there with a paddle – they'd cover them up.' They both hoot at the idea of Mayberry bearing down upon the skimpily clad girls with a paddle, chasing the young bathers away like young hens.

The two ladies hoarded a treasure-trove of island sayings. 'Poor' for 'good'. 'If someone was commenting on a pretty new dress on you might say that's ugly, which means it's a beauty.' 'Joe Blunt – when you come right out with it – straight talker'. 'Kitty Bar the Door'. 'Keeled out – flat out'. 'Narry idle – neither'. 'Cross jawing – talking back and forth.'

Stella reels off a list of words and phrases. 'Boomed off – I can't explain it.' 'Blackgun and thunder – somebody with a bad temper, a bad disposition.' 'It was a couple got married round here one time and they'd say that they was "black gun and thunder" coming – one was just as or'nery as the other.' 'Drawn off – when two people are in conversation and they're not aware of things going on around them.' 'Sing it low – keep quiet about something.' 'That lays the deck – that's an old people saying.' 'All you can say Grace over – a lot.' 'Scuppers under – on a boat they have little scupper holes where they wash their decks and the water goes overboard – somebody taking a large load would be scuppers under.'

'I don't know if I should say this,' says Mayberry, 'but we called the bone at the end of the spine the crapper bone. I went to the hospital in Crisfield and a nurse said only horses and animals – four-legged creatures – have a crapper bone.' 'Struck Poor Crooks a blow – he was a coloured man who married a white lady – the islanders tried to separate them.' 'Crippled sudd'ly – taken ill.' 'Cuter on yourself – a woman putting on makeup would be cutering on herself.' 'Tongue basting – tongue lashing.' 'Noogs are sweets.' 'Kindle up old coals – if you were friends with somebody and you kind of got on the ice or something – you fell out but you made up.'

In her book about Smith Island, Frances W. Dize portrays islanders as having five or even possibly six senses alert to changes in the weather: 'They . . . learned to use all their senses to foretell the weather: the taste of foul weather (the bitter, coppery tang that comes from the marsh in late fall, leaving its warning of unsettled conditions), the smell of rain on the way, the sound of thunder in the distance, the sight of a blue rim on the horizon, or the heavy feeling of lowering pressure that comes on before a storm.'

Thundersqualls breed easily in the wide mouth of the Potomac, and stormy weather can catch a man in a boat unawares, consequently signs of change are to be looked for and respected. The weather is all in the waterman's way of life.

As I met people on the island I set about collecting their sayings about the weather:

'Lots of dragonflies is a sign of an east wind.'

(Waverley Evans)

'Lots of flies presage a change in the weather.'

(Carl Tyler)

'If you seen the sun come up and it looks like somebody sat on her and flattened her it'll be slick calm all day, but if she come up just round as a ball you're going to have some wind.'

'Red sky at night, sailor's delight: red sky in the morning, sailor's warning.'

'Them big mosquito hawks: there's a northeaster when they start flying around.'

(Elmer Evans)

'When the air smells of watermelon there's sharks in the water.'

(Captain Larry of the *Jason II*)

'Mosquito hawks or skeeter hawks [two local names for dragonflies] – flying around is a sign of a change in the weather.'

(Stella)

'A ring around the moon it means rain.'

(Mayberry)

As I was leaving the two delightful old ladies, Stella pressed me to stay for just a few minutes more so that she might read me a poem by her stepmother, Livia Marsh . . .

There's a beautiful little island
Between Tangier Sound and Chesapeake Bay
It is called Smith Island
It is part of our good U.S.A.

There are three parts to this island
We're proud of them as can be
Ewell, Rhodes Point and Tylerton
Each a separate community

We have three lovely churches
In which to sing and pray
And a wonderful pastor whom we all love
To keep us from going astray

107

At Ewell there is a sacred spot
Which everyone holds dear
That spot is the old camp ground
Meetings are held once each year

It's sort of like a homecoming
Where old friends meet once more
And our voices blend together
In the gospel songs of yore

Visitors come from far and near
Our island for to see,
There enjoy our style of cooking
And our hospitality

Our livelihood comes from the water
But we don't plant the sea
God does all the planting
And he supplies our need

Some folk think us peculiar
To live in this isolation
But to us who live here
It's the best place in the nation

We're all God-fearing people
Our standard of living is high
It's a heritage left by our forefathers
And it's something money can't buy

We live like one big family
We love our fellow man
When anyone is in trouble
We lend a helping hand

I'm proud to live on this island
Between the Sound and Bay
This little bit of heaven
Smith Island, U.S.A.

Chapter 12

TO THE POINT

The land seems not to rise above the water level. Only the trees and the houses, rising on an often imperceptible base, mark limits beyond which there is no water. But even such a notion is less than true, for the inquisitive tides here poke inland behind every acre and house and forest, ferreting, rummaging, creating tiny necks, and bringing one shore so near another shore that there often seems scarcely room for the road that balances on its way.

Paul Wilstach, *Tidal Maryland*

Walking along the mile-long road that separates Rhodes Point from Ewell, the tide was slowly inundating the land with its silver tentacles of water. There are fewer than five miles of road in total on Smith. Even during this short stroll some cars passed me more than once, the joyriders out to enjoy a road which can offer few conventional pleasures of driving. There is barely enough room to pass, let alone overtake. This being Smith, each driver waves or nods, old-time courtesy at the wheel.

Pausing on One Lane Bridge, I watched the little hunchbacked herons skulking in the reeds. The water in the creek rolled away from the eyeline, a great glass python slowly uncurling. A squadron of pelicans flew over the edge of land, surveying the surf. They are a familiar sight around the island, and the eight-mile journey from the mainland will often afford grand views of pelicans resting on the tops of poles, characteristically placing their bills on their breasts.

The adult birds have lovely chestnut-brown feathers at the back of the neck trailing away to yellow, and have matching yellow foreheads to boot. The colonisation of this part of the Chesapeake by these flying mouths is a very recent phenomenon, as they only started nesting after 1990. Twenty years ago they were virtually unknown in these parts, and, much like the bald eagles and ospreys, had suffered the effects of the chemical warfare waged against the countryside in the heyday of noxious pesticides such as DDT. One of the individuals we have to thank for such changing times is Rachel Carson, who railed against such indiscriminate poisoning.

Nowadays there are some 600 pelicans around the Virginia-Maryland state line. If you include non-nesting birds and young birds, the population probably stands at around 3,000. These stupendous birds have elasticated throats and, after a successful plunge into the water, one can see the unfortunate fish wriggling and tickling and struggling inside the stretchy membrane.

The pelican's fishing technique involves scouting the surface of the water from a height, then before retracting its head and neck, folding its wings slightly and diving. It will not spend long under the water and, when it surfaces, it tilts its bill downwards to extrude a great mass of water which has been scooped up into the gigantic bill, as much as ten quarts. It then tilts the mighty bill upwards to swallow the catch, its favoured meals being finger mullet, anchovies and silversides. One staggering estimate has it that a brown pelican gan gorge its way through over a hundred pounds of fish in its first nine weeks of life.

On a small collection of ponds, which lay like a scattering of diamonds in the distance, a small flock of waders was busily needling the mud looking for invertebrates. These were semipalmated plover which cried 'too-li' as they spiralled away in tight formation, the small flock wheeling and turning in perfect synchronicity, as if the birds were briefly turned into one organism. It really was as if each bird knew when the bird flying next to it would bank and twist. This can be explained as a device by which a predator finds it difficult to disengage one individual from the flock – and yet it is more than that. The flock of birds is more than the sum of its parts. It is the finest aerobatic show; it is precision-flying, the like of which no air-force display team, for all its high-tech backup, could ever achieve.

There are a good many pines shading some of the houses at Rhodes Point. The first house I came to was surrounded by beaten-up cars in variously advanced stages of rusty dereliction, out of kilter with the pathological tidiness of the Smith islanders. Just as someone can be house-proud, so are the people of Smith island-proud. A good few houses stood empty in the town and no human voices were to be heard anywhere. It was one of those Marie Celeste moments, when you find the ship empty but there is supper laid on the table.

I strolled around the Calvary church, built in 1921. Its architecture befits simple acts of worship – a box, the simplest temple. The German philosopher Schlegel once said that 'architecture is frozen music', and this church hymned a quiet melody under the noonday sun.

The people of Rhodes Point are known by other islanders as 'cheese eaters' because of their habit of eating cheese in coffee, as compared with the 'herring hucksters' of Tylerton and the 'bean snuckers' of Ewell. There is a faint smell of liquorice in the air courtesy of the stands of fennel (which thrives hereabouts), their umbrella heads opening along most of the hedgerows. A car sticker on the windshield of a beaten-up automobile chugging past proclaimed: 'Promote catfish – run over a chicken.' Delicate terns scream as they survey the waves for a glimmer of fish, hovering momentarily before crumpling their wings and diving down. The elegant birds fluttered like butterflies above the water.

I walked past The Railway, the island boatyard, owned by the Marshes of Marsh Road. Here two boats, the Miss Yvonne and Amanda Lyn sat ignominiously in dry dock.

I had come to visit Ben Whitney, one of the oldest inhabitants of Rhodes Point. The house had that musty smell that inhabits the homes of the elderly, a compound of moth balls, dusty memories and airborne motes of skin dried to parchment. He was wearing a crisp powder-blue work shirt and $200 glasses, and is still tall and rangy despite his eighty-eight years. In the background, a radio tuned in to the conversations of the watermen on the Bay keeps him in touch with the wider world. It is his lifeline. I noticed that he also had a special radio designed to be listened to in the shower.

His walls were full of ornaments. Ben had surrounded himself with many mottoes arrayed on the wall. A Smith Island Oil Company calendar proclaimed: 'Greet the day with satisfaction and you may expect satisfaction at sunset.' There was also a print of flowers emblazoned with the legend: 'Those Who Bring Sunshine To The Lives of Others Cannot Keep It From Themselves.' And another admonition: 'I shall pass through this life but once. If there is any good I can do let me know it now for I shall not pass this way again.' Like the homes of many Smith islanders, there was a great deal of maritime memorabilia – model lighthouses, a plastic ship's wheel, and a packet of playing cards decorated with saucy models. On another wall there was a representation of a packet ship with the words 'All I ask is a tall ship and a star to steer her by.'

'I've seen it hard, so hard I wondered how I made it. I've seen it good, then seen it hard again.' But Ben, despite life's ups and downs, remains phlegmatic, as he trusts that there is a preordained reason for his reaching this great age:

'I've been kept here for some reason – I can't tell you what but there's a reason . . . My parents are dead, my wife's dead, all my wife's people are dead. I'm the only one left – my sister's dead, her children and my mother's sister and her children . . .'

Ben hasn't lived on Smith all his life. He spent thirty-two years living and working in Baltimore. 'I made money for my wife and daughter up there.'

He worked in the shipyards, places of extraordinary industry. When he started in the shipyards he toiled and sweated for a mere sixty cents an hour – 'working on anything

112

that goes inside engines, boilers, main engines.' His first pay cheque was $27 for a week's work, and he had to work Saturdays as well to get that. His father used to work on farmland for a dollar an hour.

The early part of Ben's marriage was blighted by the fallout from the Wall Street crash and the pinch felt during the years of the Depression that followed. 'We got married and I hit a tangle during the hardest times there ever was in the world, and one of the hottest times and one of the hardest times – you just couldn't make a living; you couldn't even make up expenses you couldn't do it – crabs was bringing nothing. I got married in 1937, the hardest time goin', so in '39 I went to Baltimore, where I couldn't get a job. I got broke walking around Long Dock in Baltimore. I didn't know where I was going to go. I thought, "boy this is good, I'm going to have to go to a bums' place dressed in my suit of clothes!" I don't know what guided me but at Long Dock there was a boat laying there, and the man who owned it was the one who wanted to adopt me when I was a little boy. I said I must have been guided right. I called him Captain John, and I asked him if he was going down to Smith Island and he said he was going down there in the morning. That was a break, not a penny in my pocket.'

Ben actually worked on *The American Mariner* – the 'ghost ship' that had materialised in the mist when Carl Tyler had taken me out on his boat. 'The first trial they tried her out, and she got twelve knots and the engines wide open – they were supplicating engines like the Titanic had – with those long rods – the others is turbines which are ten times more powerful. She was a half an inch out of line on her keelson so the Government got together and decided to make a training ship out of her taking people down the Bay. A lot of them got sunk and a lot of them got scrapped.'

The Liberty ships – of which 2,700 were manufactured, were completed in, on average, between forty-seven and sixty days. They formed the backbone of the American, British and European merchant fleets in the '40s and '50s, and were still used by countries in the Far East in the '60s. One of the most

113

colourful characters in the drive to mass produce a great armada of ships was Henry J. Kaiser. Despite having had no previous experience of shipbuilding, he set out to 'build ships by the mile and cut them off by the yard.' One of Kaiser's Pacific Yards in California set the world record for ship construction. The S.S. Robert E. Peary was launched on 12 November, 1942 just four days, fifteen hours and thirty minutes after her keel was laid. Nowadays only one is seaworthy – the S.S. Jeremiah O'Brien, a floating museum owned by the U.S. Maritime Agency.

During the Depression, Ben tried to get welfare, but had to take the option of joining the Civilian Conservation Corps and went to work on the great retaining wall that is the Hoover Dam.

When he came back he started crabbing and shucking oysters again. 'But the mystery of this island I can never understand – back in the old days when I was born there was all the oysters you wanted. You could run a boat across them and the shells they would cut your bottom, they were sticking up like that – people weren't eating the oysters; they weren't eating the crabs – they raised a garden and they'd eat out of the garden. Never heard of them eating the crabs. Even when I growed up we wouldn't eat them – my father never knowed one to have a mess of crabs in the house. Crabs were cheaper than dirt – crabs that big' – Ben opened out the span of his palm to demonstrate – 'you could have any size you wanted.

'In 1940 and 1942 everybody started catching crabs and picking crabs and away we went – that's when prosperous times started and everybody was making a dollar – putting money in the bank. We started to get ahead a little bit.'

For Ben, as for most other watermen, the world of the crab remains enshrouded in mystery. If there is a man who claims to understand them then he is either haplessly arrogant or just plain wrong. 'You can't understand crabs because they travel. In the fall of 1939 I was crabbing – trotlining – and by eleven I hadn't caught a crab. Something told me to go close to the bank. The tide had pushed up with a northeaster – the tide had

114

rised – and of course I went in that way close to the shallow water. I run my line down and tightened it up, you know, I made one of the best day's work I ever made in my life in two hours – I caught about five hundred rank peelers that day and everybody weren't catching a hundred. In them days they were worth about three to four cents.'

The migrations of the Bay are miraculous. Barry Lopez's description of animal movements on land is remarkably applicable to the movements of waterborne creatures. 'Watching the animals come and go, and feeling the land swell up to meet them and then feeling it grow still at their departure, I came to think of the migrations as breath, as the land breathing. In spring a great inhalation of light and animals. The long-bated breath of summer. And an exhalation that propelled them all south in the fall.' And they are not all visible migrations. The tiniest creatures can hitch rides on the various currents set up in the Bay. By moving vertically they can take advantage of different flows, southbound flows of fresh water, for example, and heavier salty water heading north.

The Chesapeake is a magnet, a larder, a crossroads and a filling station. It is a huge avian flyway, a freeway of the air. Birds come here from far-flung places. Barn swallows might travel all the way from Argentina and Chile. Canada geese might come from Canada's remote Ungava peninsula, whilst tundra swans will travel from Alaska's north slope and from the extreme reaches of Siberia, beyond the beech-studded expanses of the *taiga* region, to where the rim of the world grows ever colder.

Ben casts his mind back, his memory untroubled by having to sift through so much experience. He remembers various eras in the Bay's recent history. He remembers the coming of the artesian wells. Before that they collected rain in tanks. 'A politician came and said, "If I get elected I'm going to make sure you get some wells," to which a local woman replied, "If we don't, I'm going to come looking for you."' But came they did, in 1937. 'It's water from nine hundred-odd feet in the ground – that's good water.' Smith Island water, drawn from such deep and pure aquifers, looks like pure crystal and could quench a desert thirst.

Ben bemoans the dearth of crabs, blaming the fish. 'A lot of hardheads have got in the Bay and they're eating up a lot of the smaller crabs.' In a story related by Rachel Carson we are told how, during the Second World War, a chain of hydrophones was set up by the United States Navy so they could listen to the waters of the Chesapeake, alert, of course, to the dangers posed by German U-boats sharking into home waters. In the spring of 1942, the surface speakers gave off a strange noise, like that of a pneumatic drill tearing up a pavement. It was impossible for the scientists to discern the sound of a ship in this white noise, which transpired to be great schools of hardheads or croker on their spring return to the Bay from their wintering grounds offshore. They were then able to modify their machines to screen out the voices of the fish, which, of course, happily continued to chatter to each other.

Other fish species have gone through periods of decline. Rockfish or striped bass used to be caught in gill nets, but in the 1970s a huge decline was noticed in the rockfish population. The finger of blame was pointed at the toxins produced by coal-burning power stations and industrial dumping, although trying to identify the source of pollution in the Chesapeake is not easy as the wastewater of six states pours into the bay. So much human waste, industrial outpour, animal excrement and agricultural run-off leaches and leaks into the Chesapeake that it might be seen as a huge sink for our detritus.

Our talk turns to health – is there an elixir of youth, a secret to his longevity? He remembers ailments being treated by a few drops of British oil or even a few drops of kerosene on some sugar. Castor oil, Sloane's linament, Epsom salts and nitre – each had its place in Smith Island medicine chests during his youth. Ben remembers many people using herbal remedies – 'the best herbs were found in higher land not in your marshland'.

The old folk would make herb tea by boiling up roots, such

as cypress roots which would thin the blood. A little beech nut would also be brought into service – boiled up it would yield the flavour for chewing gum. 'If they didn't have enough cough syrup they would boil up an onion, drain it off and mix the pulp with honey and vinegar.'

Ben has also been a great fan of asparagus and eats it every day – he believes fervently that it's good for the kidneys. 'Lots used to grow around here but it's clustered all up with weeds now which have killed it. Nobody gets up and gathers it now.' When he was young he remembers children going around with big bundles to sell, each vigorously defending their patch: 'You're on my 'sparragus, you're on my 'sparragus!' they would yell. Childhood was rough – 'you never seen a penny unless you dig a great big yard up; you got a quarter or fifty cents for it.'

Ben has lived long enough to see the number of people who live in Rhodes Point dwindle to an almost unviable level. By comparison, 'when I was about four years old, we had eight or nine hundred people.'

Rhodes Point can be a lonely place, with no store, no Post Office, nowhere to meet on any day other than Sunday. 'You don't see nobody hardly at all. I listen to CBs – to the watermen out there.'

I leave the old man nursing his memories, cocooned in his loneliness, his only harvest now the crackly voices coming in from the boats in the Bay.

Chapter 13

PROGGING
AND OTHER PASTIMES

The sea provided: a barrel bursting with butter
sweating salt; sea-moulded lumps
of dark wax I still polish with; the captain's chair
at the head of our table . . .

Christine Evans 'Broc Môr'

The constant music on any edge of the Chesapeake is the lapping of the waves. Even when the water is as still as a millpond it still beats insistently and invincibly upon the shore. After a storm, some mudbank surfaces are sheared away, revealing hidden treasures, uncovered history. The rhythm of the tide is so insistent and so pervasive that the periwinkles which cling by the dozen to every stalk of cordgrass would continue to move up and down the woody stems even if they were removed from the Chesapeake. They slowly yo-yo, day by day, as an echo of ebb and flow. As the late Rachel Carson once wrote: 'To understand the shore, it is not enough to catalogue its life.'

Most lakes and coastal bays have a shoreline two, three or four times the length or width. The Chesapeake shoreline is forty times as long. It is the greatest shell and fin fish bay in north America. On average, the Chesapeake is only twenty-one foot deep, yet the variety of fish – 265 species in summer – and the quantities in which some of them occur beggar belief. In a place of such plenitude the flotsam and jetsam, the windwash and spindrift are equally plentiful and varied, so beachcombers and mudlarkers can stumble upon so many things. It has given rise to a particular kind of person – the progger, an estuarine investigator on a small and intimate scale.

The dictionary defines 'progging' as: 'to poke (as) at a hole or log; forage, prowl, wander about idly or aimlessly.' It's a very old word which originally meant to 'pick up a living by begging or thieving' which gradually came to mean 'picking up clams or oysters, or catching some fish when food supplies were low.' Progging is about chance, the luck of the tide and the assistance of the wind. Just as the word serendipity owes its origin to the chance discovery of the island of Sri Lanka by the Arabs, so does progging owe its delights to accident. The sea can wash almost anything onto the shore, at any time.

Consider the story told by one island expatriate: 'One winter, word spread over the island. Captain Ed had found a large box afloat packed with beautiful high-topped shoes in all sizes. He announced that he would give them away on a first-come, first-served basis.' There were, apparently, many Cinderella moments as the island women tried on the shoes, with the Captain joking that they must have come from the Titanic.

Ask anyone on Smith who is the most industrious progger and they'll cheerfully pipe up with the name Alan Smith. I met Alan – the 1997 Crabber of the Year – as he relaxed of an afternoon. He was tucking into an enormous carton of Salt Water Taffy Caramel Corn whilst watching television.

In common with so many watermen, Alan Smith started work at an very early age. 'At twelve years of age I had a boat of my own with a one-cylinder Falcon motor in her and I scraped her for one or two years. Then my father bought me a boat with a four-cylinder Grey. At that time, it was all one-cylinder engines – Palmers, Falcons, Fishermens and Redwings and a few more – but they were all one-cylinder engines.

'I'm almost sixty-four years of age now, and for fifty-two years I've worked on the watering. I loved it. I like the work, I love my job and I always liked to catch crabs and fish and oysters. It's been a good life – it's hard but it's been a good life.

'I was once a guide for a hunting lodge on South Marsh Island, working for a military bunch out of Washington D.C., and I had twenty-seven years there as head guide. When their head guide died at forty-five I took over, and I didn't realise how big the job that I was doing at the time was, but when you sit back here now and look on television, you see a lot of 'em and what position and stuff that they took in the armed forces and all, it makes you wonder . . .

'I've had secretaries of the navy, generals, admirals, commodores, you name it, all except the President – we never did have the President.' The current incumbent's face looks out from the television screen, a symbol of silver-tongued mendacity.

I asked Alan about the days when the skies darkened with great flocks of birds over the Bay.

'Wildfowl – I've seen some days in my lifetime – I don't believe I'll be exaggerating none. One day I remember in particular, it must have been hundreds and hundreds of thousands of ducks in the air. I never seen nothing like it in my life, and after that we had a great big freeze come. I guess the ducks was getting ready to migrate further south, but it seemed that all day long everywhere you looked the sky was full of 'em – redheads, canvasbacks and bluebills, pintails and mallards and all different species. Canvasbacks have really gone down in numbers but I think last year you were allowed one – that's the first time you've been able to shoot one in I guess fifteen or twenty years – they're making some comeback maybe.'

Canvasbacks not only acquire the flavour of the wild celery – *Vallisneria spiralis* – which is a favourite feed, but it has even become part of its name – *Aythya valisineria*. The rest of the name comes from the Greek and means, quite simply, water bird. The celery-loving waterbirds have declined catastrophically in the Bay over the years, due in great measure to the disappearance of enormous acreages of underwater grasses, also to pollution, although Hurricane Agnes didn't help, muddying the waters as it did.

One hopes that the fate of the canvas won't follow the same course as that of the wild pigeon, the passenger pigeon. At one time wild pigeon did quite literally blot out the sun and darken the skies, flying in gargantuan flocks. They could break down trees with the sheer weight of their numbers, but they were easily confused by torchlights and could be easily clubbed to death at their roosts. The coming of guns hastened the exit of the species from the world, and the last individual representing this once abundant bird shuffled off its perch in a zoo.

Alan Smith might have seen some mighty flocks of ducks and geese in his time but they are as nothing compared with the congregations which used to darken the winter skies, and might have flown all the way from the realms of myth. Myth, is after all, only very old gossip. They arrived in 'millionous multitudes', according to one colonist. One Robert Evelyn, exploring near the head of the Bay in the middle of the seventeenth century, estimated that one flight of duck measured seven miles in length and a mile wide, and he likened the 'rushing and vibration' of their wings to a storm coming through trees. This might be a hyperbolic flight of fancy, yet duck numbers in the Chesapeake can sometimes assume dramatic proportions.

One third of the waterfowl wintering along the Atlantic coastline choose to wing down to the Chesapeake, although some species which traditionally visited the Bay now look elsewhere for their winter fare. Following the decline of underwater grasses – which has seen 600,000 acres of submarine meadow shrink to an all time low in 1984 of 38,000 acres – tundra swans now choose to overwinter in North Carolina.

Alan is out there in all seasons, usually alone, sometimes worn out by his labours, or buffeted by the wind, or bereft of crabs, or sometimes at peace with it all. 'A good day is you go out and don't have no trouble with your motors, or you don't tear no scrape bags, or the engine don't break down and you have a good cool breeze – that's what we call a good day, and a

121

bad day would be a stormy day and some days you tear up a lot of things; sometimes it's a struggle to get home.'

Bad weather on the water can mean good luck for the progger on the rim of the land. 'Storms can bring good luck for a man. A northwest or a nor'easterly wind – any good wind, any strong wind will help.

'I like to get out and hunt for things, and it just proves to you that the Indians was here and the English were here and the Spanish were here. We find all kinds of artefacts – some things we found here goes back 10,000 years to the sabre-toothed tiger and we know that the Indians has been here that long.' The native Americans arrived as nomadic hunter-gatherers more than a thousand years before the first white settlers arrived.

The shoreline is surprisingly good for its numismatics: 'I've found some coins. I've got some in the 1600s and quite a few in the 1700s and a good many in the 1800s.' He showed me a coin marked C.R.S. from 1677, which I presumed stood for Carolus Rex Secundus.

'It's fun to get out and hunt for coins, but we hunt for a lot of different things – arrowheads, beads – and you never know what you're going to come up with – sometimes you come up with a gold coin every once in a while, not too often. In my younger days I did like to get out and hunt the wildfowl, and I always liked to go deerhunting too – I've been doing that most of my life – they seem to be real plentiful just about anywhere you go. Once in a while we see two or three on Smith. They're good swimmers, and they can get here but they don't stay here.' The deer were here in good numbers in Captain John Smith's day: he reported how driving the game intensively could yield as many as fifteen whitetail deer at one go.

Alan has amassed great boxloads of arrowheads – made from an array of materials – flint, quartz, jasper – one of which is twelve inches long. Looking around his room, you can tell he is an almost pathological collector. The walls hang heavy with decorations of all kinds, while his treasure-trove is proudly displayed around the room – flying ducks, ships' wheels,

English clay pipes, flints from rifles, a clock where the numerals are replaced by arrowheads – possibly crafted by Waverley's able hands – trading beads from England arranged on lengths of fishing twine, a carved teal, and a Susquehanna broadpoint arrowhead.

Progging is a hobby, but working the water is a living, which doesn't get any easier. 'There's more people into it, and it takes more crabs to supply the people now. A strong back and a weak mind – that's what makes a good waterman. A good waterman – you've got to love what you're doing and you have to put in a lot of hours, but for them that sticks in there and grinds at it they'll do the best. You can't fool around.

'I'm just about ready to hang it all up. Maybe I'll work till I'm sixty-five. I've got about a year and a half to go. I may sell my boat, the Hester Lee, or I may give it to one of my grandchildren – there are four boys and one girl. About a couple of them will probably work on the water, but a couple of them might get their education and do something else. I think they would be wise to get education and move on to different things, because who knows what the water business will be like – they put so many restrictions on you now you don't know sometimes if you're going to make it or not. I guess down the line, the community won't be able to sustain itself. The people that lives on these islands – there's no farming – just about one hundred per cent of their income comes out of the water except a few that owns the gas stations and schoolteachers and a few different jobs. Tourism's all right but from what I see of it they don't spend very much money in the community, they just come and go.

'What we know about the crab is very little. What we know is that they produce a lot, but it's a lot of just about everything eats a crab – all your different birds, all your different fish. They say one crab spawns millions – which I believe – and some of 'em survives. Crab life is short – about eighteen months to two years is about the life of a crab. I'm sixty-three year old – I've seen more little crabs the last three or four days than I've ever seen in my lifetime. It's a good sign. If the cold winter don't get them, or the fish don't eat 'em up.'

123

The blue crabs of the Chesapeake have declined. The Bay once produced more blue crabs than any other body of water on the globe, and even after sharp falls it still produces almost half of the harvest of the entire United States. By the early 1990s the Gulf of Mexico produced more crabs at a time when the Bay's own harvest had fallen from an average of forty-seven million pounds to thirty million pounds in weight. The arguments over the precise cause or causes still flare up from time to time. In 1996, the National Oceanic and Atmospheric Administration reported that the blue crabs were not overharvested and pointed to a natural cycle as the probable cause. Other theorists suggest that, commercially, more females have been taken out of the water in past years. Tropical storm Agnes, which destroyed ninety per cent of the Lower Bay's eelgrass – ecologically, both a nursery and kindergarten – was similarly blamed.

Measures were taken in the two states of Virginia and Maryland from 1994 onwards to shorten the crabbing season. Vigorous lobbying for a ban by the Chesapeake Bay Foundation resulted in further restrictions in the fall of 1995. Signs started popping up on Smith which declared that 'Smith Island's way of life will soon be over due to the Chesapeake Bay Foundation. Please do not support them.' Foundation property was vandalised and an arsonist set light to one of their outbuildings. The Foundation responded by threatening to close its centre at Tylerton which draws 2,500 middle and high school students to the island and helps to ensure the survival of the daily ferry service.

It was seen by many as a David-versus-Goliath contest, and there are still small ripples of ill feeling. At the time, one of the watermen, Glenn Evans, summed up the situation as follows: 'They're hurting us real bad. They're regulating us off the island.' You will still hear the word 'regulation' used much as some people use vigorous Anglo-Saxon curses in order to vent their spleen. It is easier perhaps to stop a few watermen catching crabs than to address the titanic scale of pollution of the Bay, from farm waste to city detritus. In most situations to be made in the employment market the world over, where an argument sets potential gains against environmental damage, it's usually the case that employment wins, often hands down. The world still works in the short term, and the notion sustainability is frequently no more than a placebo. Yet, in the case of the Smith islanders, it seems that it is easier to squeeze the small man rather than question the ways in which big cities dispose of their waste. That is not the way to safeguard the ways of the watermen or blue crabs for future generations, but perhaps our myopia doesn't allow us to see that far.

Alan continues to catch and eat crabs. 'I don't think we ever get tired of 'em – we don't eat them all the time but quite often, about once every two weeks, something like that. Fish you will get tired of if you eat it very much, but crabs – seem like you never get tired of 'em – or I don't. Softshell crabs and shrimp is two of the best things comes out of the water.' Diligent progger Alan Smith knows more than most.

That wildily inventive writer and denizen of the Chesapeake, John Barth, progs a little. In *Once Upon a Time*, he lists the 'washed-up aquatic dead' he finds on the creek side:

> *blue and horseshoe crabs, young turtles strangled on promotional or party balloons, sunfish, bluefish, white and yellow perch, rockfish, spot, croaked croakers, giant carp, stranded Chrysaorae and moon and winter jellies, clam and oyster and mussel shells . . . In a week's visit, our brace of grandchildren can assemble on the bulkhead a virtual museum of tidewater natural history; their grandparents find at least as fascinating the miscellaneous man-made dreck. Observes one of Samuel Beckett's derelict beachwalkers, 'I never needed a board but there it was, I had only to stoop and pick it up.' We have a basement hoard of perfectly usable lumber salvaged from our marsh after storms, flood tides, or extended absences; a bin of nylon and polypropylene lashings chafed through at one end but otherwise sound; a shelf of Styrofoam flats and buoys come loose from crab traps and eel pots out by the channel and beyond.*

As I walked from Alan Smith's house, alongside Tylerton's main channel, two birds sprang straight up from the water and cannonballed away down a gut, then gained height and began circling. They were black ducks. American black ducks are like wet mallards rolled lightly in a bed of soot before being freed, their plumage dark-dabbed and mottled. In flight, white linings and deep violet wing panels – called speculae – flash like sudden semaphore, and the sheer unexpectedness of a pair rising from a cordgrassed creek was exhilarating, the male croaking hoarsely, the female quacking like her farmyard cousin. They were very dark overhead. It looked as if their shadows alone had taken wing.

Fortuitously, and a tad ironically, duck blinds – hunters' hideaways – have proved to be a popular nesting site for black ducks. In a study conducted in the 1950s, it was found that seventy per cent of black ducks nested on blind roofs. Three hens went so far as to lay their clutch of eggs in deserted great blue heron nests that had been constructed in the upper reaches of pine trees, almost a hundred feet above ground level.

During the 1930s, severe droughts and the agricultural drainage of the prairie potholes of the Dakotas and nearby Canadian Provinces drastically reduced the black duck population. Between 1956 and 1958, an average of 110,000 black ducks were to be found within the Chesapeake Bay watershed. Between 1996 and 1998, the number had plummeted to an average of 24,000.

On Smith, the fact that the island vegetation is mainly made up of salt-marsh plants – some eighty per cent needlerush – is not conducive to the nesting of black ducks – and the decline in widgeongrass meadows is believed to have had a far-reaching detrimental effect on the species.

That wonderful contemporary chronicler of the Chesapeake, the journalist Tom Horton, remembers his father

> *returning with a 100 pound burlap sack full of canvasback and redhead ducks. Dozens and dozens of duck and geese. It*

was nothing for me to pick up thirty or forty black ducks,
fifteen geese in a single night. We had duck hunting you
couldn't buy today. They seemed inexhaustible. Now, they
may not be around in the twenty-first century because of
both overhunting and habitat degradation. Rockfish, our
bread-and-butter fish, we used to catch by the dozens,
occasionally by the hundreds. I remember rockfish fighting
in the rivers, thrashing in the shallows on Nanticoke in their
spawning run, so many of them they made an enormous
noise.

In stark contrast with the vocabulary of abundance and
variety which used to apply to the Bay, the words used now –
depletion, emptying, disappearance, extinction – sound the
death knell for this great snaking stretch of water unless
greater care is taken to protect it.

Luckily, much of the wildlife habitat of Smith Island is
protected. The Martin National Wildlife Refuge, encompasses
the northern half of Smith Island and covers some 4,500 acres.
Bald eagles visit regularly, while rookeries of herons and egrets
on Watts Island number 1,200 birds, on a site which is little
more than 125 acres. From a distance, adult male and female
great blue herons appear to be identical, but close and careful
scrutiny permits the identification of individuals according to
their facial markings, as is the case with swans. Peregrine
falcons have been encouraged to nest by erecting nesting
towers and by the introduction of young birds to the area. This
is one of the bird world's most spectacular athletes. High
above its hunting territory, it can look too remote to be
menacing, yet once it has spotted its prey, it arches through
the sky in a breathtaking descent, attaining an estimated speed
of 180 miles per hour. Even on routine patrol, their flickering
flight is a delight.

The marshes have their own soundscapes, one of the
principal components of which being the songs of the red-
winged blackbirds, those Marsh Dandies, flashing their red
epaulettes, and singing 'okalee'. The red-winged blackbird is
possibly the most abundant bird in North America. But

127

perhaps *the* sound of the marshes is that of the clapper rail, or marsh hen – secretive and skulking, but betraying or rather announcing its presence in the stands of cordgrass with a loud 'chac chac chac' or 'cac cac cac'. Awkward in flight, but strong of leg, the clapper rail is a progger of distinction. It is also a gamebird – shot usually after a high tide driven by north winds pushes it within sight of a hunter's gun. Sometimes it is killed at low tide when the birds feed on the mud flats – for it feeds mainly on fiddler crabs.

The architecture of birds' nests is difficult to comprehend – how can a bird which has never watched another bird build a nest – and has never therefore learned by example – build one from scratch? How can the clapper rail not only work out the structural engineering which allows it to create a relatively solid affair out of the marsh materials on hand, but also furnish it with a canopy to conceal the eggs from the sharp eyes of scouting fish crows, and also provide a ramp facilitating easy entrance and exit? The nest itself is just above the level of high tide, although sometimes things go amiss and the nest is washed away. Such is the productivity of the clapper rail, however, that clutches usually number nine or ten eggs, with second clutches – following fish crow predation or flooding by high tide – averaging five eggs.

On Smith there are few paths, and the freeway that links Rhodes Point with Ewell, cutting across great swathes of marsh and crossing deep-watered guts, can be a limited experience for the ornithologist on foot. Especially as the heat increases, and the birds hunker down in shady places and save their songs for later. But even on stiflingly hot sparkling summer afternoons, butterflies flutter by – Smith has its share of hairstreaks, skippers and swallowtails, the tiny beats of their wings underlining the stillness of the afternoon.

One afternoon, with sunlight on the channel at Tylerton, I borrowed a canoe from my hosts at the charmingly named bed and breakfast, the Inn of Silent Music, slid its sharp prow into the water, and cast off from the little jetty in front of the house. A local crabber had just brought in some croker for our supper. I waved goodbye to my host LeRoy Friesen, who was taking his serrated gutting knife to the mess of fish, and struck out for open water.

There was one of those Galapagos moments when I realised that some of the wildlife became more trusting now that I had taken to the water. Small wading birds needled the silt on the edges of the channels, and egrets stretched out their pipe-cleaner necks, unblinking eyes alert to the movement of the merest fish gill in the shallows. I aimed for some loblollies, but the water wound in such a labyrinthine way that plotting a straight course in my canoe was impossible. Tiny crabs fiddled away into bore holes in the mud.

Sea nettles pulsed in the water. The nettle may have the sort of Latin name that would prove a mouthful even to a classical scholar – *Chrysaora quinquecirrha* – yet it has a beauty too, the medusa bell beating as it expands and contracts. Few people are aware of the fact that a jellyfish is in fact a large member of the family of floating plankton and in the Chesapeake float they do, much to the consternation and irritation of swimmers and waterskiers who, in high summer, when the populations of the sea nettles peak, have to relinquish the Bay to the silent invaders. They are truly the stuff of B-movie science fiction – opportunistic and carnivorous, they drift until unwitting and unfortunate prey comes their way. The prey rapidly becomes entangled in a net of tentacles, each bearing a series of stinging cells which act very much like stun guns. The stinging cells release little darts which can easily penetrate the softer parts of human skin. Caught by the jellyfish, then dazed and confused, the hapless creature passes through long mouth lappets into the mouth. Take a good look at the centre of the jellyfish bell and you might well see an undigested shrimp or small fish.

One small fish in particular should be singled out, simply because it is one that doesn't mind the ghostly embrace of the sea nettle. Young harvestfish or butterfish are able to swim in an out of the long tentacles like floating half dollars, having developed an immunity to their poison. Some spider crabs also

129

live in symbiosis, catching a ride on the bell, or even sometimes hollowing out a travel compartment in it.

By the end of summer, the sea nettles have gone but there is one other species of jellyfish, the lion's mane or winter jellyfish, which can sometimes be as abundant as the sea nettle, but as these orange-brown relatives only appear in the Bay in late November, growing to adulthood through the winter, they are much less conspicuous than their summer cousins. The other occasionally abundant species is the moon jellyfish which, as its name suggests, has a flat, white bell. It can appear in great numbers in late summer, while the mushroom cap jellyfish, normally a sea creature, can drift in throughout autumn and early winter.

I drifted onwards in my canoe into the heart of the marshes, the cordgrass growing around me up to seven feet tall. There was a rich smell in the air, putrefaction, rot, mud-methane and brackish water – that soup of sustenance for so many creatures of such wetlands.

Wetlands such as these have disappeared at a devastating rate. The U.S. Fish and Wildlife Service estimates that they were disappearing at a rate of 4,500 acres in the Chesapeake Bay between 1982 and 1989. By 1989, about 1.7 million acres remained.

Overhead, some barn swallows, known on Smith as shanty birds – because there are far more shanties than barns for them to nest on the island – scattergunned away, their gaping mouths trawling the air for insects.

Then, on a dead branch, I saw it – a bald eagle, which would have been worth canoeing all the way from Kamchatka to see. It held the thick branch beneath it like a match, standing straight as a sentinel. I have always loved eagle tales, such as the probably apocryphal one about the three-year-old girl who was snatched by an eagle in Norway in the 1930s and lived to tell her tale for a suitable number of kroner. In the Scottish Orkneys, fear of the sea eagle was so socially ingrained that anyone who shot one was entitled to receive a hen from every household in the community. A comparable vermin control

130

system in the Faroe islands, known as *nevtollur*, or beak tax, stipulated that any son killing this particular species would be exempt from paying the levy for the rest of his life.

Although the bald eagle has been the national emblem of the United States of America since 1782, it has not been without its dissenters. Benjamin Franklin was among those who railed most stridently against it:

> I wish the bald eagle had not been chosen as the representative of our country, he is a bird of bad moral character, he does not get his living honestly, you may have seen him perched on some dead tree, where, too lazy to fish for himself, he watches the labor of the fishing-hawk, and when the diligent bird has at length taken a fish, and is bearing it to his nest for the support of his mate and the young ones, the bald eagle pursues him and takes it from him . . . Besides he is a rank coward; the little kingbird, not bigger than a sparrow, attacks him boldly and drives him out of the district. He is therefore by no means a proper emblem for the brave and the honest . . . of America . . . For a truth, the turkey is in comparison a much more respectable bird, and withal a true original native of America . . . a bird of courage, and would not hesitate to attack a grenadier of the British guards, who should presume to invade his farmyard with a red coat on.

That's as maybe, but the bird in front of me, immobile, a symbol of latent power and seemingly lazy flight, was a commanding presence, a king for the marshlands.

The big bird receded as I stroked my way forward, along channels where the water was only inches deep, my paddles stirring a thick soup.

I came to standstill. The canoe rocked back and fore as I identified some of the plants growing on the water's edge – groundsel and marsh elder. I am not the only Welshman to botanise in the Chesapeake. One of the early colonists was a man called Hugh Jones – a young assistant to the pioneering Welsh naturalist Edward Llwyd. Llwyd – a correspondent of the great Swedish taxonomist Linnaeus – was keeper of the prestigious Ashmolean Museum in Oxford, from where he despatched collectors to investigate the flora of America. Hugh Jones volunteered to go, but in order to have money to live on he was ordained as an Anglican priest – a sort of office of convenience – and was sent to the Chesapeake in 1697. He sent back case after case of specimens, seeds and live plants, many of which did not survive the journey. Hugh Jones's rate of collecting slowed after a couple of years, much to his patron's consternation. What happened was this. Life was testing and often isolated in the nascent Maryland. Set against a backdrop of trials and tribulation his parishioners' spiritual needs were very intense. They cried out for help and Jones, slowly but surely, took to heart his role as cleric. His demanding role took it out of him and he became ill. His letters after 1699 become truly heartrending to read. He died of TB, and was buried beneath the chapel at Christchurch on the Patuxent river.

His plant collection lives on in the Sloane Herbarium. The cardinal flower that Jones collected is still red on its ancient page after three centuries. You can still see live cardinal flowers each summer in the cypress swamp at Battle Creek, just a few miles' walk from today's Christchurch, where Jones is buried. Jones and the other collectors probably preserved about a quarter of the plants which constituted Chesapeake's original flora.

The wind ushered me along the guts, with no need for the paddle. Herons flew in loose formation overhead.

A great blue heron plunged its head into the water, its sharp bill reminding me of a Scottish dirk, that flat stabber's dagger. The list of food that disappears down the throat of the great blue herons is a fairly representative snapshot of the more plentiful chapters of the natural history of the Chesapeake: mummichogs or common killifish, striped killifish, small crabs, frogs, young snakes, mice, grasshoppers, silversides, Bay anchovies and juvenile menhaden and crayfish.

There are eight other members of the heron and egret family that patrol the Bay, standing stock-still until the fateful lunge.

The smallest is the little green heron, dapper and seemingly hunchbacked, which often perches on fallen trees. On Smith, there is a favourite site near the waiting-bridge where the birds can perch on driftwood fishing verandahs, taking full advantage of their stalking brethren by fishing deeper water. Other relatives have different strategies – cattle egrets are newcomers to America where they have expanded at a rapid rate. Originally European birds, they have flown the south Atlantic to Brazil and then steadily colonised their way up through central America, and then started burgeoning colonies throughout the southern States. They are often to be found in association with beasts of burden, horses and oxen and cattle, of course – running around energetically in pursuit of reptiles, insects and other small animals.

At the end of the day Chinese brush strokes bring grey into the candyfloss pink of the sunset and the sun is a silk swirl of red and ultraviolet. Daylight leaches away. It is the time when foxes sneak out of their lairs and pad around the marshes. Red foxes, which routinely swim across the tidal guts of Smith, have a five-star menu of delicacies available to them on the island. This changes according to the season, with all manner of eggs – from terrapin to oystercatcher and black duck – or young herons and egrets displaced from their nests, marsh-nesting birds, injured birds, Norway rats on spoil sites, carrion washed up on beaches, persimmon fruits and berries of wild cherry, and possibly a blue crab or fiddler crab dinner, eaten *en plein air.*

That evening I ate indoors and went for my usual supper at Rukes Seafood Deck – an eatery made out of wood and corrugated iron which is at least a hundred years old. The islanders were using 'backward' or 'upside-down' talk, also known as 'talking over on the left' and one fellow diner was saying 'that's no film' when what he meant was that it *is* a film, it is a good film. Jennings Evans had pointed out a few examples as we listened to the watermen's recorded conversations one afternoon. They might as well have been speaking Mandarin, Serbo-Croat, or one of those clicking languages spoken by bushmen in Africa for all that I understood of their banter. Jennings thinks it might be used in part to bind people together, whilst helping to exclude others. After all, as someone once said, on Smith, 'they have made an artform of vagueness'.

Jennings explained some of the sayings. 'There he's saying "It won't take anything to get him to laugh," which means it will take a lot of comedy to get him to laugh – probably no comedian on earth could do it.' Another voice said 'It ain't nothing is it?' which actually meant that there was a problem.

Jennings also pointed out the phenomenon known as 'code-switching', which happens when an islander switches from backward to forward talk, usually in deference to a bewildered stranger. But he also warned that some things are said because of another form of speech altogether, what he calls Lazy Speech. 'We don't say "ing" at the end of a word because it tires the face to say it.'

Another interesting linguistic feature of the island is the proliferation of nicknames – Licking Billy, Nut Sundae, Juke, Toesy, Spot, Tank, Gadget, Peewee, Barcat. Carl Tyler's father is called Tapeworm because he can't keep still. There is a man called Hoss named after the character in the television series *Bonanza.*

And past generations have made their contributions to the names of the places on Smith – Apes Hole, Hucksters Gut, Eagle Hammock, Solomons Lump, The Wading Place, Puppy Hole, Horse Hammock and Twitchy Cove.

I imagined Silas Wegg, the man with the wooden leg, who looks after the junk shop in Dickens's *Our Mutual Friend*, would have felt very much at home here. Rukes is jammed to the rafters with stuff: tins of pumpkin soup, a glass-topped display cabinet full of intricately carved duck decoys, crates of soda, two large refrigerated units, a titanic chest freezer, a porcelain figurine of a ten-pin bowler in one of those heroic poses one normally associates with Russian workers in the early part of the twentieth century. But instead of a stone hammer he has a large bowling ball and is standing next to an outsize bowling pin. There is some 'White House' cherry pie filling, a china mallard duck, a Lilliputian child's desk so small the seat is only a foot above the floor, a white lifebelt, a large preserved crab, a table made of eighteen pieces of driftwood, a miniature oyster dredge, a brass deer, a model giraffe, a Christmas tree in a basket – complemented by an outsize Yuletide decoration made of pine cones – bottles of apple cider vinegar, stacked packets of Jell-O and saltine crackers, a model wildfowler, bamboo wind-chimes, conch shells, a silver candelabra, higgledy-piggledy piles of books including multiple copies of the *1979 Year Book of World Events*, a video cassette called *Moses in Egypt: Daniel in the Lion*, tins of cranberry sauce, very old, dusty bottles of sea-sickness pills, a groaning shelf full of Chesapeake lighthouses, sailing ships, a rack of necklaces, one display case full of old drinking glasses, another containing a grand array of kitsch nick-knacks, including a set of dolls' furniture complete with real mirror, a plastic unicorn, an Easter egg with a bunny sat astride it, some needlework, a Slush Puppie dispenser with a gigantic cup revolving on top, a washboard, a can of clam chowder. Beyond, in the open-plan kitchen, various animated women are beavering away, making crab cake sandwiches. Rukes looks like a progger's paradise, a treasury of found things, never to be sold or abandoned.

Chapter 14

WHAT THE FUTURE HOLDS

*If the sea doesn't cover us over and if people keep
eating crabs and if God's willing there'll be a Smith
Island for maybe a hundred years.*
Smith Island waterman

The new millennium opened as a crack of daylight over the
South Sea islands of Kiribati in Micronesia, islands doomed to
be erased from the tinily dotted map by the middle of the
twenty-first century.

The rate at which the sea level is rising in the Chesapeake
and along the mid-Atlantic coast is twice the worldwide
average. During the last century, the waves rose approximately
one foot as they lapped against the Maryland coast. Scientists
disagree about the underlying reasons for this inexorable rise.
Some blame land subsidence: others wag accusing fingers at the
changing climate and its effect on the volume of the ocean, and
the extent to which they can accommodate polar meltwaters.

Each wave changes the land. There are some experts who
believe that the Bay first came into being about thirty-five
million years ago with a bang and not a whimper, as a huge
meteor – at least a mile in diameter – turned into a gargantuan
fireball and smashed into what is now known as the lower
Chesapeake Bay, a little west of Cape Charles, Virginia, at the
tip of the Delmarva peninsula. This would have caused a
tsunami wave as high as fifty feet whilst shards of glass from
crystallised molten rock would have fallen down as solid rain
as far away as Barbados and Texas.

But the waves that change the land nowadays are causing
alarm. At a 1996 conference called 'Chesapeake Bay at the

Crossroads', some 140 scientists, government officials, property owners and other interested parties met at Washington College in Chestertown, Maryland. Smith Island is not the only area affected, for erosion of beaches and wetlands has claimed a third of the entire Blackwater National Wildlife Refuge during the past few decades. In Somerset County, farmed land is fast becoming salt marsh, or simply land too salty to cultivate effectively. The best, or worst projections, have it that global warming will most probably lead to a rise of about two feet in the next century, or even three or four feet.

There are eight federal agencies involved in studying the Bay, in addition to state agencies, and universities and legislatures.

The Bay and its tributaries are thought to be losing an average of a foot of shoreline each and every year, and some 45,000 acres have tumbled into the water during the last hundred years. A study by the U.S. Corps of Engineers found that, since colonial times, erosion has wiped twelve of the thirty-five islands of the middle Bay and Eastern shore off the map, a loss of 10,500 acres. During the next century, according to Professor Michael Kearney of the University of Maryland, sea levels will rise three feet, compared with a rise of four inches to a foot in the last century.

Smith Island is being eaten away at a rate of seven feet a year. Not only is the sea rising to claim the land but the land is also sinking – only a fifth of an inch a year but, as Jennings Evans pithily puts it, 'that's twenty inches every hundred years. We can't spare too many inches.' Building on a marsh is like building on a sponge.

John Barth has penned some phlegmatic lines on the subject in his novel *Once Upon a Time*: 'But then, before very long in geological time, the melting polar caps will drown our floodplain altogether, reconfigure the Chesapeake and rearrange the whole East Coastscape. Meanwhile, praise be, the coast is the coast, Bay Bay, creek creek, and our marsh is marsh, which we prize not least for the wealth of stuff we have found in it and its margins.'

Smith is being lost – inch by inch and minute by minute – for time marches on, and time and tide wait for no man. Smith Island is a rich habitat for man, a place trapped in time, yes, but also a place with a future. The population may have been cast into parlous, possibly final decline, yet several babies have been born there recently and in the gurgling cries of the newborns there is hope.

Some of the island's young people are pessimistic nevertheless. As young Craig Evans told me recently, the U.S. Army Corps of Engineers has already been at work on Smith. It dredged a Federal Navigation Channel and the silt material was placed along the Eastern shore of Smith at a place called Twitch Cove. Eelgrass was then planted to provide a nursery habitat for juvenile fish and a shedding area for blue crabs. Geotubes – large, sand-filled tubes – were used to protect the site from the action of the waves. It's a start. But could you surround the whole island?

In the Bay watershed, a population which soared to the 14.7 million residents of 1990 will become 17.4 million by the year 2020. The William Preston Lane Jr. Bridge built between Annapolis and the Upper Eastern shore in 1952, and the Chesapeake Bay Bridge Tunnel, a 12.5 mile long complex of tunnels and bridges, completed in 1964, have opened up the Eastern shore to commuters. Condominiums have sprouted.

Smith is still at one remove from that sort of development. Here is an island community, where one island visitor musing on the possibility of leaving observed: 'I can't quite tell whether they're behind or ahead of us.' Not for nothing has the twentieth century been referred to as the Age of Extremes – and there is something so very moderate about Smith.

Smith, by dint of being an island, has kept the twentieth century at bay. No Walmart, no multiplex cinemas, no eight-lane freeways, burger franchises, neon signs, spray-can graffiti, designer drugs, accelerated living, Generation X, soulless malls. Rather, it is a custodian of the old ways, and though it can seem to be a museum in a way, the people here are very real and the work is very hard and their worship is very sincere.

Perhaps science cannot halt the slide of Smith into the sea, and perhaps the State's will to save it simply isn't there. But what will be lost is a place where tradition is an anchor, where language has a rich brightness so that you want to hold certain words up to the light to see them glint, where chocolate cake must be made with seven layers on pain of death. Here the clocks run slow, the dolphins surface, the perfect crabs taste as perfect as the last mess of perfect crabs you ate, and the herons glide over the marshes, and the sun refuses to set . . . not quite yet, not quite.

BIBLIOGRAPHY

Books

Barth, John, *The Tidewater Tales* (Baltimore, 1987).

Barth, John, *Once Upon A Time* (London, 1995).

Bode, Carl, *Maryland: A History* (New York, 1978).

Carr, Morgan, Russo, *Colonial Chesapeake Society* (1988).

Carson, Rachel, *The Sea Around Us* (London, 1952).

Chowning, Larry, *Harvesting the Chesapeake* (Centreville, 1990).

Davison, Steven G. et. al., *Chesapeake Waters: four centuries of controversy, concern and legislation* (Centreville, 1997).

Dize, Frances W., *Smith Island, Chesapeake Bay* (Centreville, 1990).

Earle, Swepson, *The Chesapeake Bay Country* (Baltimore, 1923).

Foster, Sally, *The Private Life of Smith* (New York, 1977).

Hawke, David, *The Colonial Experience* (Indianapolis, 1966).

Horn, James, *Adapting to a New World* (Williamsburg, 1994).

Horton, Tom, *Bay Country* (Baltimore, 1987).

Horton, Tom, *An Island Out of Time* (New York, 1996).

Horton, Tom & Harp, David W., *Water's Way* (New York, 1992).

Horton, Tom & Harp, David W., *Swanfall: Journey of the Tundra Swans* (New York, 1991).

Jacoby, Mark E., *Working the Chesapeake: Watermen on the Bay* (Maryland, 1991).

Johnson, Paula J., *The Workboats of Smith Island* (Baltimore, 1997).

Lippson, Alice J. & Lippson, Robert L., *Life in the Chesapeake Bay* (Baltimore, 1997).

Meanley, Brooke, *Birds & Marshes of the Chesapeake Bay Country* (Centreville, 1975).

Paterson, James Hamilton, *Seven Tenths* (London, 1992).

Poole, Alan F., *Ospreys: A Natural and Unnatural History* (Cambridge, 1989).

Roger Tory Peterson, *A Field Guide to the Birds of Eastern and Central North America* (Boston, 1980).

Schubel, J.R., *The Life and Death of the Chesapeake Bay* (Maryland, 1996).

Stevenson, Mary Ann, *True Story: My Youth on Smith Island, Memories* (1985).

140

Tate, Thad W., & Ammerman, David L., *Chesapeake in the Seventeenth Century* (New York, 1979).

Touart, Paul Baker, *Somerset: An Architectural History* (Maryland Historical Trust, 1990).

Warner, William, *Beautiful Swimmers* (New York, 1994).

White, Christopher P., *Chesapeake Bay: Nature of the Estuary, A Field Guide* (Centreville, 1989).

White, Dan, *Portraits of the Chesapeake: Crosscurrents in Quiet Water* (Dallas, 1987).

Whitehead III, John Hurt, *The Watermen of the Chesapeake Bay* (Centreville, 1979).

Williams, J.P. Jr., *Chesapeake Almanac* (Centreville, Maryland, 1993).

Wilstach, Paul, *Tidewater Maryland* (Indianapolis, 1931).

Wright, Louise B., ed., *Everyday Life in Colonial America* (New York, 1965).

ARTICLES

'Past is Prologue', Kent Mountford, *Bay Journal* 7 (1 March 1997).

Crisfield & Smith Island Newsletter, Spring 1977.